A WEEKEND PROJECT BOOK

PLAYHOUSES YOU CAN BUILD

INDOOR & BACKYARD DESIGNS

By David & Jeanie Stiles

FIREFLY BOOKS

A FIREFLY BOOK

Published by Firefly Books Ltd. 1999

Fifth Printing 2001

Library of Congress Cataloguing-in-Publication Data available.

Cataloguing in Publication Data
Stiles, David R.
Playhouses you can build : indoor & backyard designs

Includes index.
ISBN 1-55209-315-8

1. Children's playhouses – Design and construction – Amateurs' manuals.
I. Stiles, Jeanie, 1944–   . II. Title.

TH4967.S75 1999   690'.89   C98-932688-8

Published in Canada in 1999 by
Firefly Books Ltd.
3680 Victoria Park Avenue
Willowdale, Ontario M2H 3K1

Published in the United States in 1999 by
Firefly Books (U.S.) Inc.
PO Box 1338, Ellicott Station
Buffalo, New York 14205

Design: Susan McClellan
Production Editor: Kimberly DuMond
Cover photograph: Richard W. Brown
Plants and garden furniture on cover courtesy of Horsford's Nursery, Charlotte, Vermont
Printed and bound in Canada

*The Publisher acknowledges the financial support of the
Government of Canada through the Book Publishing Industry
Development Program for our publishing activities.*

To our daughter,
Lief Anne,
the inspiration
for our book

Acknowledgments

Many thanks to our editor, Sandy Taylor,
for her invaluable editing skills and to Judith and Nat Sobel
for introducing us to her. We would also like to thank Kimberly Du Mond
for the many long hours she spent editing the text and illustrations
and Barry Estabrook for his enthusiasm
and continuous support.

CONTENTS

Introduction

With a designer for a father and an actress for a mother, our daughter, Lief Anne, never had to worry about being entertained. Over the years, while David was writing books about tree houses, forts, huts and hideaways, our daughter was surrounded by creative activities and enthusiastically took part in trying out our new designs. Consequently, the property surrounding our renovated barn in East Hampton on Long Island was always filled with kids who gravitated to our place to play.

We have swings inside and outside the house. The bedroom on the second floor has folding shutters, which creates a perfect stage for theater productions and puppet shows. For years, our dinner parties ended with a play or musical, performed by Lief Anne and the children of our guests.

Outdoors, there were always several on-going projects. One of our main goals has always been to keep the playhouses unobtrusive, nestling them between trees and working them into the environment. Because of our interest in architecture, children and entertainment, it seemed natural for us to write a book on playhouses—not just playhouses for the country, but also city playhouses.

Our daughter was born in New York City, and once, to our amazement, after an idyllic summer in the Hamptons, she asked us (at the age of three), "When are we going back to the city?" Manhattan, after all, has Central Park, filled with climbing statues of Alice in Wonderland, the Dairy, an Adirondack gazebo, a model boathouse and a children's zoo filled with playhouses of all shapes and sizes. In the winter, after a heavy snow, the plows conveniently push the snow into gigantic

mounds, which are easily transformed into snow houses. The sheep meadow in Central Park is a great place to sled and build a snow fort.

A playhouse can be anything that you and your child dream up—the range of designs is unlimited. Those included in this book can be reproduced as described or simply serve as suggestions to inspire creations of your own.

The appeal and importance of playhouses is universal. They are used by children not just for playing in, but also for "role playing." In a playhouse, children can exercise their judgment and play adult roles. They can practice sharing and experiment in a more private, "child-sized" environment—one that they have more control over. Through imaginative play, children learn how to understand themselves and the world around them. When children play with each other, they are unconsciously practicing skills that will help them later in life, like leadership, cooperation, communication and organization.

A playhouse can be a small-scale version of a "grown-up" house (like the Traditional Playhouse on page 57), or as fantastic as the mind allows (like the Fiberglass Whale Playhouse on page 39). Today, as more and more families have both parents in the work force, helping a child plan and build a playhouse is a wonderful way to spend time together, creating something that will have long-lasting benefits. Parents who nurture their children's sense of play and respond to their ideas while planning and building a playhouse can give them a sense of accomplishment, self-confidence and security. In a playhouse, children are the producers, the directors and the actors.

SECTION I

PLAYHOUSE PARAPHERNALIA

SAFETY

SAFETY IS THE MOST IMPORTANT CONSIDERATION when planning and building a playhouse. In this book, we have taken certain liberties to make these structures as safe as possible. For example, in many cases, we specify shorter nails than are conventionally used. This is done so that when nails are hammered into the roof or walls, their pointed ends will not protrude through the ceiling and interior walls. If there are times when a nail does stick out, it should be hammered so that it bends over and is flush with the surface.

Since lumber and plywood are used in most of the projects, be sure to watch out for splinters on railings and other surfaces that are exposed to a lot of handling. Take time to sand these until they are smooth and, for extra protection, cover them with two coats of polyurethane. In addition, round off and sand any sharp edges and corners.

Always clean up your building site at the end of each day, making sure to retrieve any nails, screws and bolts that are left on the ground. Pick up all tools and store them in a shed, workshop or other protected area. Secure the lids on cans of paint and polyurethane and clean all paint brushes thoroughly. Replace the tops on tubes of glue and construction adhesive, containers of contact cement and other similar supplies.

DOS:
- Do keep a first-aid kit handy for the unavoidable scrapes and nicks!
- Do let your children get involved in the playhouse design and give them certain tasks to do, based on their age and ability.

DON'TS:
- Don't let children operate power tools.
- Don't operate electric tools in wet conditions.
- Don't use a two-prong extension cord.
- Don't leave tools on top of a ladder.
- Don't step on a rung of a ladder above where the ladder rests on the roof of a playhouse.

BEFORE YOU BUILD

BEFORE YOU CHOOSE A PLAYHOUSE TO BUILD, consider the following questions:

- Where will it be situated?
- Will my neighbors complain?
- How long will it take to build?
- Will I have to buy expensive tools?
- How much will the materials cost?
- Can it be converted to another use when my child outgrows it?
- Can it be moved?

Unless you are building a playhouse for indoor use, most are constructed in the backyard, partly for privacy and protection, and sometimes because of a zoning law prohibiting "accessory buildings" from the front yard.

Some localities require you to file for a building permit; most, however, consider a playhouse a temporary structure, not built for habitation, and do not require a permit for any accessory buildings under 36 square feet.

When you are deciding on a location for the playhouse, select a relatively dry, sunny spot and build on slightly elevated ground, where rainwater does not collect. After you have finished building, plant grass around the structure so the ground stays dry and so mud and dirt aren't tracked into the house. A good project for your kids might be to plant bulbs or grow a strawberry patch or pumpkin vines in front of their playhouse.

For those of you with nearby neighbors, there are other considerations. What may seem like a beautiful playhouse to you and your child might be just the opposite to your neighbors. To avoid any difficulties, take your playhouse plans to your neighbor and get his or her approval before you begin to build. Another option is to build your playhouse where your neighbors can't see it, or build it with your neighbors (if they have kids) and let your kids practice sharing it.

Some playhouses will take only a a short time to

build, while others, such as the Traditional Playhouse and the Fiberglass Whale Playhouse (see pages 57 and 39, respectively), will require at least two weekends. A lot depends on your carpentry skills.

Another factor to consider when selecting a building project is your tool inventory. Don't be discouraged if your inventory is small or even nonexistent. If you don't want to invest a lot of money in tools, check to see if there are places in your area where you can rent them—it is better to rent a good-quality tool than it is to buy a poor-quality one. Another option is to have the lumberyard precut your wood.

If you do opt to buy, make sure you purchase good tools. I like to buy myself a new tool for every major project I build—a reward for "doing it myself." If you plan to do a lot of cutting with a portable electric circular saw, invest in a carbide-tooth blade, which will ultimately save you both time and money.

LUMBER

THE COST OF LUMBER HAS ALMOST DOUBLED since I began writing this book; consequently, it is difficult to predict how much a particular playhouse will cost. Your best bet is to take the materials list at the beginning of each project to your lumberyard and ask for a quote. If the quote seems high, do some comparative shopping at one of the home centers in your area. We don't recommend using salvaged wood unless it is clean, dry and free of defects, such as large knots and nail holes. It is often more trouble than it is worth.

If you have not done much carpentry, here are some helpful hints to read before you begin a project.

When buying lumber, you should know that the measurements given are not the actual dimensions. They refer to the dimensions of the lumber before it is dressed and kiln-dried by the sawmill. For example, a 2x4 does not actually measure 2"x4", it measures 1½"x3½", and a 2x12 measures 1½"x11¼".

Lumber is sold in 2' increments. Always take a tape measure with you to the lumberyard so you can check the actual length of a piece of lumber before you buy it. Hold the board up to your eye and look down the length of it to see if it is warped. Also look for loose knots or checks (splits) in the lumber. Remember that clear lumber (free of knots) is much more expensive than #2 grade lumber (with knots). One 8' piece of clear 1x10 can cost as much as a bottle of champagne, so be selective! Take your time picking through the lumberyard's piles. Sometimes, you can find pieces of wood in the #2 grade piles that are almost free of knots and that sell for one quarter the price of clear lumber.

For most of the playhouses in this book, the lumber size given in the materials list refers to the length at which lumber is sold, not the cut length needed for the project. One exception is the Log Playhouse, which gives both the size to order and the finished, or cut, size.

USING AN ELECTRIC CIRCULAR SAW

CUTTING WOOD SMOOTHLY AND ACCURATELY IS essential to good carpentry and makes the whole job of construction much easier. Before you make your final cuts, practice sawing on scrap wood to get used to the heft and feel of the power tool. In addition:

- Always wear eye protection whenever you are working on a building project.
- Find two solid supports, such as sawhorses, to rest the lumber on while you are cutting. Never cut the lumber between the two supports, however, as this will cause the saw blade to bind and kick back suddenly.
- Use a speed square to mark where you will be cutting.
- Provide electric power to the saw using a grounded (three-prong) plug. Make sure the cord is out of the way of the proposed cut.
- Before starting the saw, place the saw blade on the waste side of the cut line. Rest the

NAILS & SCREWS

1" 2" 3" 4" 5"

1 ½"
4d FINISHING NAIL — use to nail small boards together, especially where the nail will show

1 ¼"
3d SHINGLING NAIL — use for cedar shingles; use a shorter nail with a wider head for asphalt shingles

2"
6d GALVANIZED SIDING NAIL — use to nail siding to studs

2"
6d COMMON NAIL — use to nail ¾" lumber to framimg

3"
10d COMMON NAIL — use for framing and for toenailing studs to plates

3 ½"
16d COMMON NAIL — use when nailing through a 2x4 into the end grain of another piece of lumber

5"
40d COMMON NAIL — use to nail heavy beams to each other or into trees

1 ¼" DRYWALL SCREW — used extensively to join wood. Do not use in exterior conditions

2" GALVANIZED DECK SCREW — the coarse thread holds well in heavy lumber

½"x4" LAG SCREW — use to join lumber to trees and posts

5 ½" CARRIAGE BOLT — use to bolt lumber together

> NOTE:
> The same length/size can apply to different types of nails, bolts and screws.

speed square on the top edge of the piece of lumber, butting it up against the base of the saw. Holding the speed square tightly against the wood, start the saw and push it through the wood, keeping the saw base pressed against the speed square while you are sawing.

• Important: Make sure that the waste part of the lumber will fall down and away from you when you are finished with the cut.

EASY-TO-MAKE WINDOWS

THIS SINGLE-SASH OR BARN WINDOW IS SHOWN in several playhouses in this book. It can be custom-ordered from your lumberyard, or, if you own a table saw, it can be made at home in about an hour's time and for less than $10 in materials.

The reason this window is so easy to make is because it uses only one piece of glass (or plastic) instead of several small window panes. The muntin bars are applied to both sides of the glass or plastic to give the impression of truly divided lights.

Since there is so little wood needed, select only the best available clear stock. If the window you plan to make is smaller than 2' x 3', buy 2x2 cedar from your lumberyard and use it to make both the window frame and the muntin bars.

STEP ONE
FRAME

Using a table saw, cut the four pieces for the window frame to the required length. Cut 45-degree bevels on each end.

Locate the points where you want the muntin bars to join the frame and make ⅜"x⅝" dado cuts.

STEP TWO
MUNTIN BARS

To make the muntin bars, cut a piece of 2x2 in half, lengthwise, with a table saw. Place one of the two pieces cut-side down on the table saw, and make another cut lengthwise; repeat with the other piece, so that you have four identical ⅝"x⅝" pieces.

Test to make sure that they fit perfectly into the dado slots cut in Step One.

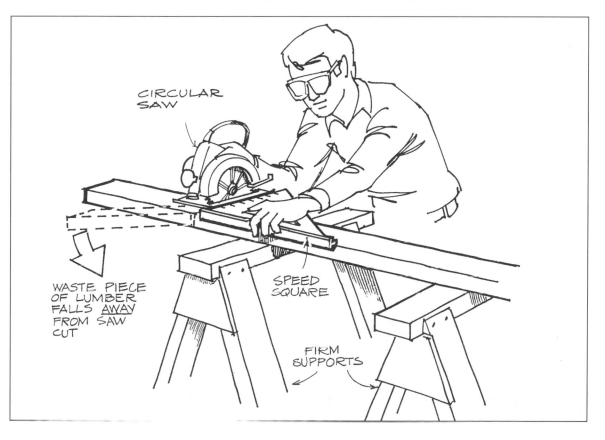

CIRCULAR SAW

WASTE PIECE OF LUMBER FALLS AWAY FROM SAW CUT

SPEED SQUARE

FIRM SUPPORTS

STEP THREE
CORNER JOINTS

To join the window frame pieces together at the corners, cut a 2" slot in the end of each 2x2 (see illustration). Make sure each slot is exactly in the center of the wood. Cut four 2"x2" right triangles out of a scrap piece of plywood; they should be the width of your saw blade. Trial fit them into the corners.

STEP FOUR
WINDOW GROOVE

To hold the window glass (or plastic), make a ⅜"-deep groove in the center of the inside face of each piece of the window frame. Cut a piece of ⅛"-thick glass or plastic to fit into the groove. To cut plastic, score it first using a utility knife, then place it over a sharp edge and snap it apart. To cut glass, use an inexpensive glass cutter and use the same technique.

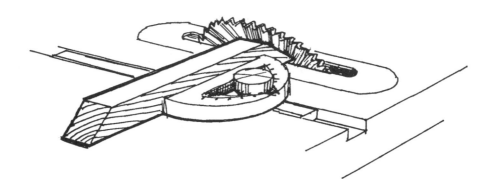

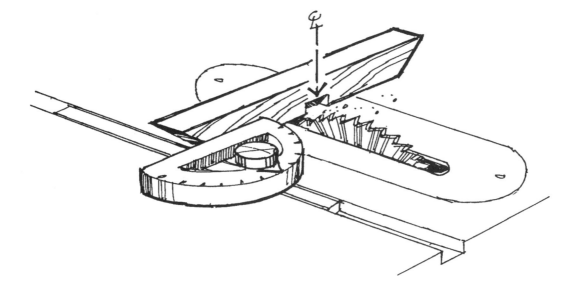

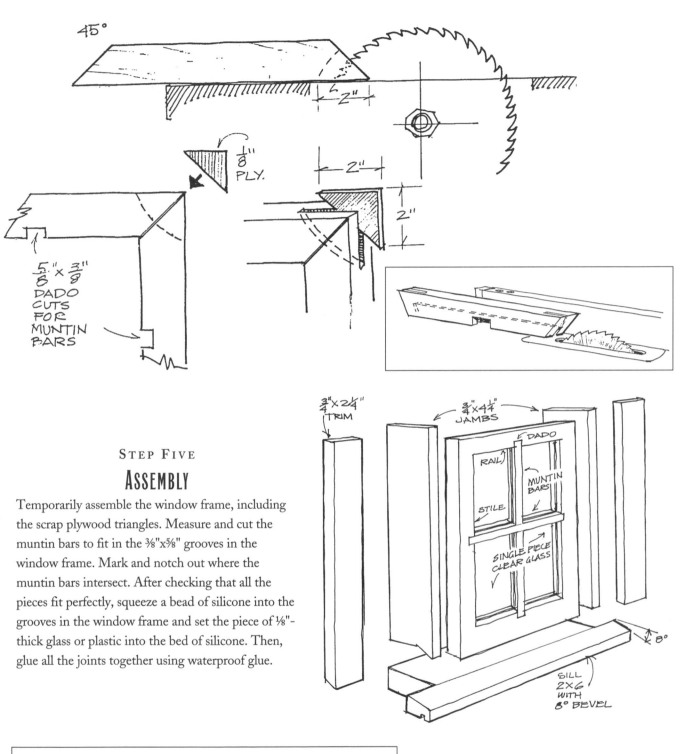

45°

⅛" PLY.

2"

2"

2"

5⁄8" x 3⁄8" DADO CUTS FOR MUNTIN BARS

3⁄4"x2¼" TRIM

3⁄4"x4¼" JAMBS

DADO

RAIL

MUNTIN BARS

STILE

SINGLE PIECE CLEAR GLASS

SILL 2X6 WITH 8° BEVEL

8°

STEP FIVE

ASSEMBLY

Temporarily assemble the window frame, including the scrap plywood triangles. Measure and cut the muntin bars to fit in the ⅜"x⅝" grooves in the window frame. Mark and notch out where the muntin bars intersect. After checking that all the pieces fit perfectly, squeeze a bead of silicone into the grooves in the window frame and set the piece of ⅛"-thick glass or plastic into the bed of silicone. Then, glue all the joints together using waterproof glue.

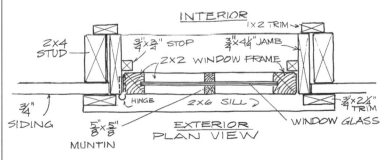

INTERIOR

2X4 STUD

3⁄4"x3⁄4" STOP

3⁄4"x4¼" JAMB

1x2 TRIM

2X2 WINDOW FRAME

HINGE

2X6 SILL

3⁄4"x2¼" TRIM

3⁄4" SIDING

5⁄8" x 5⁄8" MUNTIN

WINDOW GLASS

EXTERIOR PLAN VIEW

NOTE:
If the window is going to be painted, a more professional appearance is achieved by painting the muntin bars before installing them over the glass.

Maintaining, Cleaning, Decorating & Recycling

It is important to have good ventilation in a playhouse. It not only helps create a healthy atmosphere, but it also discourages the growth of mold and mildew. Instead of covering the space underneath the eaves with wood, either leave it open or—even better—cover it with metal screening stapled to the bottom ends of the rafters. The screening will allow for a constant flow of fresh air, and at the same time will keep out mosquitoes, wasps and other insects.

Encourage your kids to keep their playhouse somewhat organized and neat. To make this easier

for them, provide a "sweep hole" in the floor. This is done by cutting a 4"x 12" section out of the floor and reattaching it with two hinges. Place a cardboard box, which can be easily removed and emptied, inside the hole so your kids can sweep dirt, leaves and candy wrappers down the hatch. Keep a small broom in the corner of the playhouse so it is readily available.

In addition to hours—and years—of fun, a playhouse provides kids with a wonderful opportunity to practice recycling and to become more environmentally responsible. For example, playhouse furniture, shelving and storage units can be fabricated out of recycled materials: A discarded small wire spool from the telephone company can be used as a table (see p. 122), tree stumps can serve as stools and used bricks or large rocks with flat tops work as bases for tables and benches. Old packing crates also make nifty chairs and tables. Kids can organize a project by going to neighbors' houses and collecting unwanted

materials. A mosaic of varied tiles, for instance, could be laid over wooden planks for a fancy floor.

Use recycled magazines, comic books or baseball cards to create "decoupage wallpaper." Kids will love gluing their favorite pages onto the playhouse walls and covering them with varnish or polyurethane. If the playhouse has electricity, make a fortune-teller lamp by draping plastic beads over the sides of an old lampshade.

Save cans with interesting labels, coat them with varnish and use them to store everything from marbles to crayons, pens and pencils.

Our daughter used her playhouse to recycle all the wonderful shells and beach glass she had collected and stored away in boxes. She glued shells to the wall and created beach collages to give the illusion of a seaside playhouse.

You will find that once kids have their own playhouse, they will never run out of decorating ideas, and most of them can be done without extra expense, simply by recycling things found around the house or given away by neighbors.

Many playhouses can be converted to other uses after your child outgrows them. In fact, it is a good idea to plan a playhouse with this in mind. Our daughter's tree house, for example, now serves as a storage place for swimming pool equipment, inner tubes and other items. A friend of ours stores firewood in his child's former playhouse, while other neighbors have recycled theirs into bicycle or garden sheds.

PLAYHOUSE PROJECTS

CARDBOARD PLAYHOUSE

AGE
RANGE
3 TO 6

HIS CLASSIC CARDBOARD-CARTON
playhouse can be made in just 30 minutes and costs almost nothing. It is created from a discarded refrigerator carton, which can usually be obtained from appliance stores or residential building sites. It's a wonderful Saturday-morning project and is especially rewarding for children, because they can do all the decorating and much of the designing of the windows and doors. We cut out pages from an old wallpaper sample book and glued them to the inside walls and ceiling. For a soft floor covering, use carpet samples, which can be found at many carpet and rug outlets.

If the cardboard playhouse loses its appeal, it's easy to redecorate it or to simply make a new one.

MATERIALS

1 used refrigerator carton
non-toxic white glue
2"-wide brown paper tape

paint, wrapping paper,
wallpaper samples,
colored paper, etc.

TOOLS

utility knife
straightedge
paint brush

STEP ONE
SETTING UP

AFTER YOU BRING THE CARDBOARD CARTON HOME, decide on a good location for the playhouse, one where your child feels comfortable and where you can still keep an eye on him or her. Using a utility knife, remove the top flaps of the carton and discard them.

STEP TWO
ROOF

WITH A STRAIGHTEDGE AND PENCIL, DRAW A LINE down the middle of the front of the carton. Make a mark ⅓ of the way down from the top of the carton on each corner. Using a utility knife, score a line (a to a) across the side of the carton, making sure not to cut all the way through the cardboard, and fold that section inward. Do the same on the opposite side (b to b).

Mark and cut off the top four corners of the front and back of the carton where they extend beyond the newly formed roof.

Glue and tape the edges of the roof together. Wide brown paper tape is preferable, but any wide tape will do.

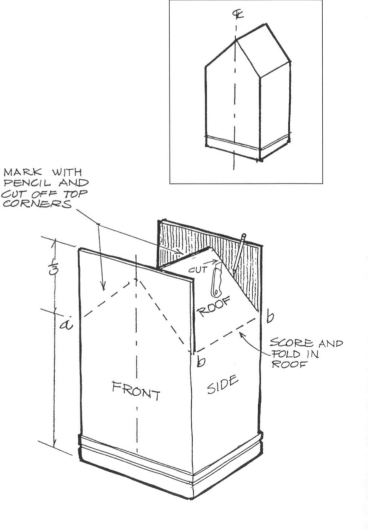

MARK WITH PENCIL AND CUT OFF TOP CORNERS

CUT

ROOF

SCORE AND FOLD IN ROOF

⅓

a

b

b

FRONT

SIDE

STEP THREE
DOOR

TRACE THE OUTLINE OF THE DOOR OPENING ONTO the front of the carton. Score the left side of the door (making sure not to cut all the way through), so that it will act like a hinge. Cut out the rest of the door and fold it open.

Mark and cut a small hole for the handle and a heart-shaped peephole for peering out—good for checking on parents!

STEP FOUR
WINDOWS & DECORATION

MARK AND CUT WINDOWS ON EACH SIDE OF THE BOX and above the front door so they fold out to form shutters. (Cut down the centerline and across the top and bottom, but only score the sides.)

Decorate the playhouse with whatever materials you have around the house—water-based paint, wrapping paper, wallpaper samples, colored paper, stickers, ribbons and hard candies. Our daughter decorated the inside of her playhouse with posters, photographs and drawings that she had done at school. The ceiling can become a private planetarium by sticking glow-in-the-dark constellations and stars onto it.

The cardboard playhouse is an ideal place to play, make plans or just daydream.

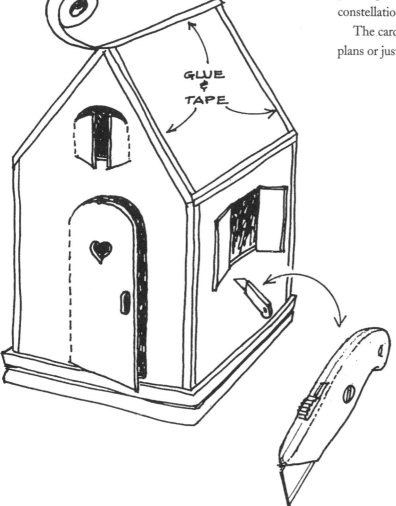

GLUE & TAPE

PLAY CUBE

INSTEAD OF BUILDING A SEPARATE PLAYHOUSE
for each fantasy situation, try creating one with four different sides. Your child can move from playing fireman, to shopkeeper, to magician or puppeteer, to mailman. As well as providing different situations for role playing, the play cube enables children to exercise other skills, such as math and writing. In the "store," kids can learn to add up groceries and make change; in the "post office," they can weigh packages. The "theater" can be used for plays, puppet shows or magic productions, which inspire children to design hand puppets and write their own scripts.

This playhouse is a great way to keep kids busy during rainy or cold days. It is easy to assemble and can even be roped together by a child, which will give him or her a sense of accomplishment. The rope corners provide a safety edge, and the simple design enables you to disassemble the play cube and store it flat when it is not in use. This is a playhouse that appeals to children of many ages.

MATERIALS				TOOLS
Quantity	**Description**	**Size**	**Location**	tape measure
2	¼" tempered Masonite panels or tempered hardboard	4'x8'	sides	square
2	1x4 T&G #2 pine	24"	vertical guides	portable electric jigsaw
	yellow glue			portable electric circular saw
1	1x2 #2 pine	8'	stops, shelf lips	clamps
2 cans	shellac-based white		exterior	V.S.R. drill
	white sealer			¾" spade drill bit
1 pint	denatured alcohol			paint brush
4 cans	enamel spray paint		exterior	marker pen
	clear & colored contact paper			matte knife
	touch-up enamel spray paint*		graphics	extension cord
	rub-on pressure-sensitive letters			
	leftover fabric		theater curtain	
36"	wood dowel	½"	theater curtain	*Touch-up enamel spray paint can be purchased at auto-supply stores
2	brackets		theater curtain	
1	¾" A/D ply.	4'x4'	ledges, shelves	
	masking tape	2"-wide		
1 qt.	polyurethane paint		ledges, shelves	
50'	polypropylene rope	½"		

STEP ONE

PANELS

MAKE THE SIDE WALLS OUT OF TWO SHEETS OF 4'x8'x¼" tempered Masonite. Be sure it is tempered: Tempered Masonite is very dark brown and smooth on both sides, so paint adheres to it much more readily than it does to untempered Masonite.

Cut out four rectangular panels 42"x48" using a circular saw. Stack them together like a sandwich and secure them with several clamps. Draw an arc with a 2½" radius on each corner and round off the corners with a jigsaw. While all four pieces are still clamped together, use the electric drill with a spade drill bit to bore ¾"-diameter holes, 6" apart and 1½" in from the side edges, to accept the ropes later. The top and bottom holes should be 3" from the top and bottom of the panel. Cut the openings for each of the four panels with a jigsaw according to the plans.

Make the firehouse doors out of leftover Masonite. Using a jigsaw, cut two 10"x20" panels and drill ¾" holes 6" apart to serve as rope "hinges."

On the inside of the post office side, glue and clamp 1x4 vertical guides to secure the grille. Next, cut the ¼"

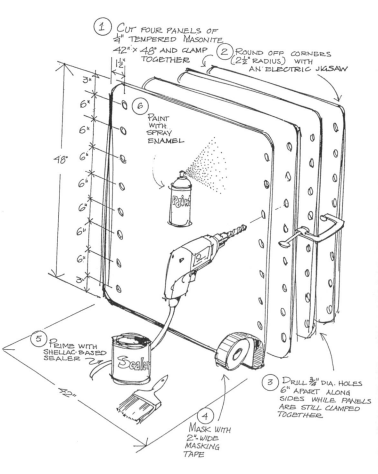

1 Cut four panels of ¼" tempered Masonite 42" x 48" and clamp together

2 Round off corners (2½" radius) with an electric jigsaw

6 Paint with spray enamel

5 Prime with shellac-based sealer

4 Mask with 2"-wide masking tape

3 Drill ¾" dia. holes 6" apart along sides while panels are still clamped together

stops out of 1x2 and glue them into the groove at the bottom of the tongue & groove 1x4s.

Then, cut the grille for the post office panel, also using leftover Masonite. Cut out each slot by drilling 1" holes 10" apart and cutting out the strip between the two holes using a jigsaw. Remove the clamps from the guides and slide the grille into the slots from above.

STEP TWO

PAINTING

BEFORE PAINTING, CHECK THE SURFACE TO BE SURE IT is free of dust and blemishes and cover the sides where the holes are with masking tape. (The rope that holds the corners together would eventually mar the paint if this area were painted.) Prime the outside surfaces with a shellac-based white sealer. Unless you use spray paint, you will need denatured alcohol to clean your brush or roller. This type of sealer dries quickly and seeps into the Masonite, leaving a flat smooth surface.

Spray each side of the cube with a different color of enamel paint. Using spray paint eliminates the messy bother of cleaning the brush four times and lets you do a much more professional-looking job. In addition, spray paint usually dries within minutes, whereas some brush-on

enamels can take days (depending on the moisture in the air), even though the label says "quick-drying."

STEP THREE

DECORATING

USE YOUR IMAGINATION WHEN DECORATING THE SIDES. Anything goes! Bear in mind, however, that it's very difficult to paint a straight freehand line with a brush. A good solution is to buy a few yards of clear contact paper, remove the protective backing and press the paper down where you want your graphics. Use a marker pen to sketch your graphics directly onto the clear contact paper, and use a matte knife to cut out and remove the letters.

Cover the surrounding area with newspaper and spray the cutout portion of the contact paper with touch-up enamel paint. Choose an accent color that stands out against the color of the panel. Then, peel off the contact paper. For smaller lettering, use rub-on pressure-sensitive letters. For other decorations, cut stars, hearts and other shapes out of colored contact paper and stick them onto the playhouse.

The theater curtains can be made out of any leftover fabric. We used velvet, which looks great, and sewed the curtains around the wood dowel.

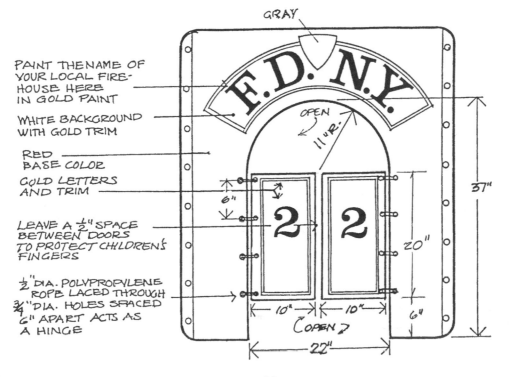

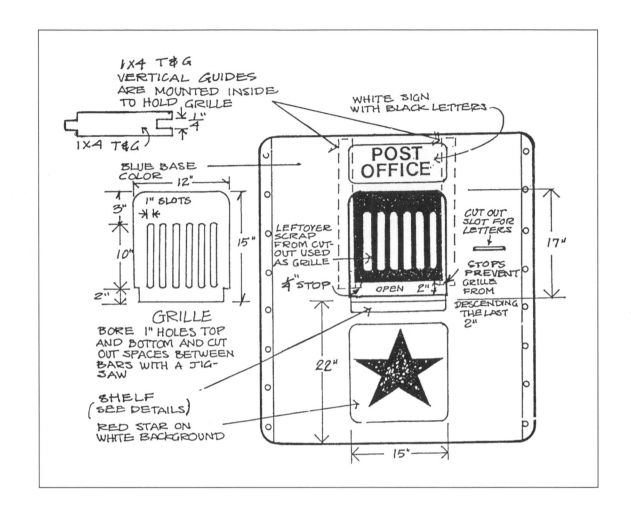

1X4 T&G
VERTICAL GUIDES
ARE MOUNTED INSIDE
TO HOLD GRILLE

1X4 T&G

WHITE SIGN
WITH BLACK LETTERS

BLUE BASE
COLOR

12"

1" SLOTS

3"

15"

10"

2"

GRILLE
BORE 1" HOLES TOP
AND BOTTOM AND CUT
OUT SPACES BETWEEN
BARS WITH A JIG-
SAW

SHELF
(SEE DETAILS)

RED STAR ON
WHITE BACKGROUND

POST
OFFICE

LEFTOVER
SCRAP
FROM CUT-
OUT USED
AS GRILLE

¾" STOP

OPEN   2"

CUT OUT
SLOT FOR
LETTERS

STOPS
PREVENT
GRILLE
FROM
DESCENDING
THE LAST
2"

17"

22"

15"

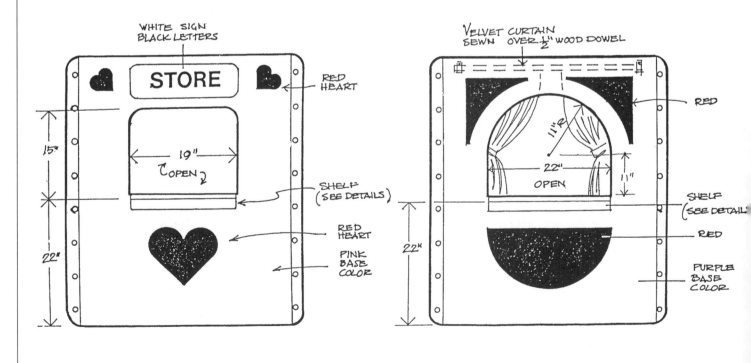

WHITE SIGN
BLACK LETTERS

STORE

RED
HEART

15"

19"
OPEN

22"

SHELF
(SEE DETAILS)

RED
HEART

PINK
BASE
COLOR

VELVET CURTAIN
SEWN OVER ½" WOOD DOWEL

RED

11"R

22"

11"

OPEN

SHELF
(SEE DETAILS)

RED

PURPLE
BASE
COLOR

22"

STEP FOUR
SHELVES & LEDGE

CONSTRUCT THE SHELVES AND STORAGE LEDGES OUT of ¾" plywood, making sure to sand all the edges smooth. All the shelves have a lip made out of 1x2s that fits into the ¼"-thick bottom edge of the window panels. Cover the shelves and ledges with three or four coats of polyurethane.

STEP FIVE
ROPE

CUT THE 50' LONG ½"-DIAMETER ROPE INTO TWO equal pieces. Starting at the bottom corner of two adjoining sides, lace the rope through the predrilled holes up to the top corner, diagonally cross it over to the opposite top corner and continue lacing downward. Tie the rope off at both bottom corners. Do the same for the other adjoining corners. The rope forms an X for a roof, which not only adds rigidity to the play cube, but also creates two lines from which stage sets can be hung, using clothespins or large clips.

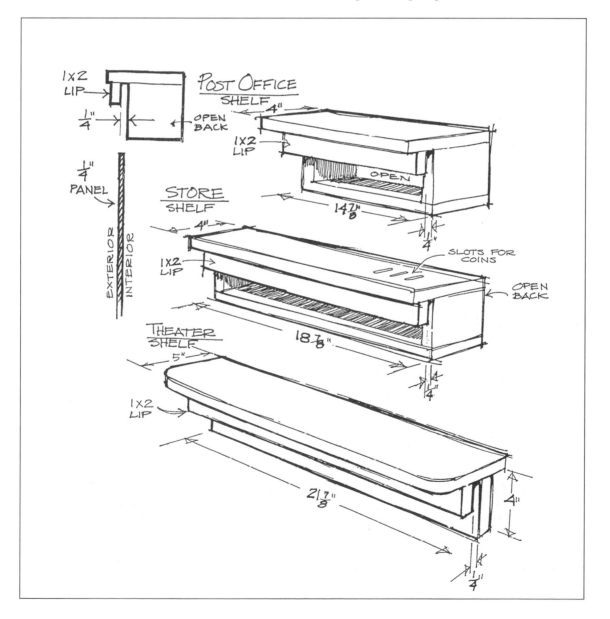

GINGERBREAD HOUSE

I DESIGNED THIS GINGERBREAD PLAYHOUSE
for The Town School in New York City, which was planning a Christmas performance of *Hansel and Gretel*. Sincc it was a class project, the kids sat down with me and described exactly how they wanted their gingerbread house to look. The set design, prop building and rehearsals were all coordinated to be finished in time for the Christmas production. Upon completion of the playhouse, we celebrated with a pre-performance party, complete with gingerbread cookies.

This playhouse is made out of plywood, and because it is less than 4' square, no interior framing is necessary. Its small scale makes it just right for young children, and after your kids outgrow it, it makes a great doghouse for a canine with a sweet tooth.

MATERIALS

Quantity	Description	Size	Location
3	⅜" ext. A/D ply.	4'x8'	floor, side walls, roof, dormer, chimney
2	2x2 P.T. lumber	8'	floor frame
	rocks or bricks		base
2	¾" ext. A/D ply.	4'x8'	front wall, rear wall, dormer, chimney
1	1x3 #2 pine	8'	door stops, window stops, chimney trim
2	¼" ext. A/D ply.	4'x8'	roof shingle panels, vergeboards
1	2x2 #2 cedar	8'	vergeboard blocks
2 pairs	black strap hinges	6"	window, door
4 pairs	galv. butt hinges	1½"x1½"	windows, door
6	black handles	4"	front door, oven door
	various colors of enamel paint		walls
	white glossy enamel paint		roof panels
	clay, play dough, durable candies		walls
	non-toxic white glue		
1 box	galv. deck screws	1¼"	
1 lb.	galv. siding nails	2½"	
1 lb.	galv. common nails	8d	
1 lb.	galv. roofing nails	1"	

TOOLS

tape measure
hammer
hand saw (cross cut)
utility knife
½" chisel
rasp
string
framing square
speed square
level
nail set
extension cord
portable electric jigsaw
V.S.R. drill
Phillips head screwdriver bit
¼", ⅜" & ¾" spade drill bits
⅛" drill bit
portable electric circular saw
cookie cutters
paint brush

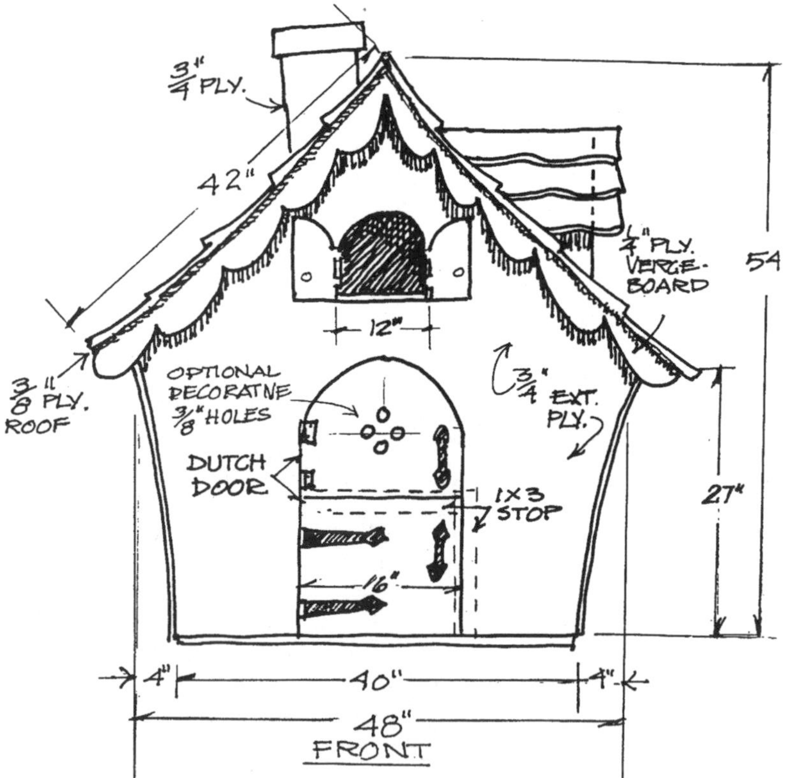

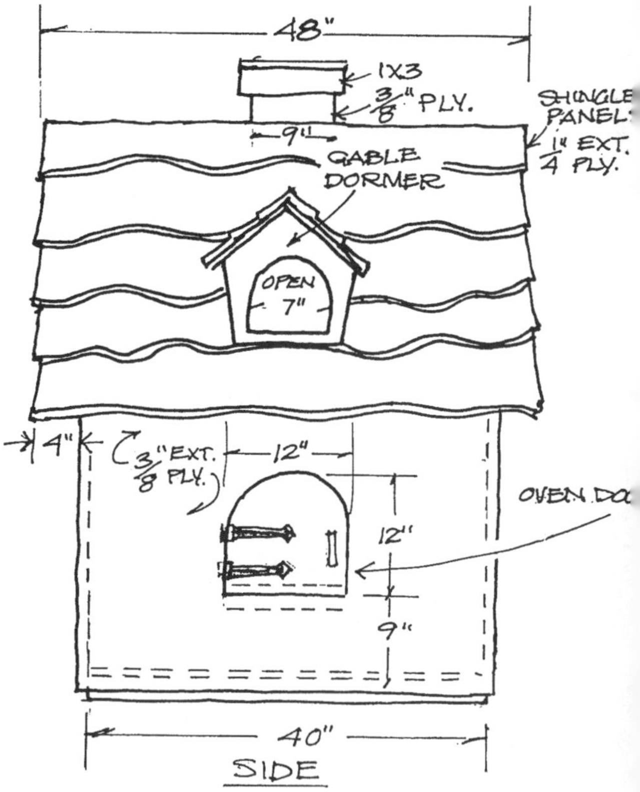

FRONT

SIDE

STEP ONE
BASE

IF YOU ARE BUILDING THIS PLAYHOUSE OUTSIDE, select a site that is level and remove any roots and rocks. Make a floor by cutting a 40"x40" square from a ⅜" plywood panel. To form the frame, use a circular saw to cut two 40"-long pieces of 2x2 pressure-treated lumber and three 37"-long pieces. Nail the plywood floor to the frame with 8d nails to complete the base. Position the base on the prepared site and level it by placing rocks or bricks under the corners.

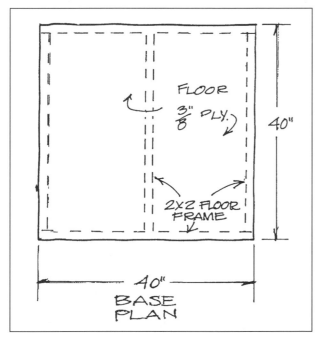

STEP TWO
WALLS

THE FRONT AND REAR WALLS ARE CUT OUT OF THE ¾" plywood panels. Use a jigsaw and follow the dimensions shown in the plans. Notice that the walls of the playhouse are splayed out 4" and are slightly curved. Draw this curve by hand or bend a thin piece of ¼" wood, position the edge against the top of the plywood and trace the curve with a pencil. Do the same for the curve of the roof.

Cut the side walls out of ⅜" plywood, following the dimensions shown in the plans.

STEP THREE
DOORS & WINDOWS

A SIMPLE TRICK THAT CAN SAVE YOU A LOT OF TIME and trouble is to attach the hinges before cutting out the whole door or window. Draw the outline for the window and door as shown in the plans. Using a jigsaw, cut the hinge side of the window or door first.

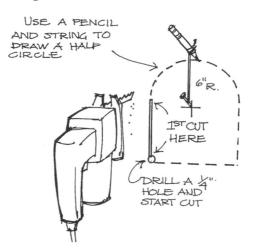

Before cutting any more of the window or door opening, screw on the hinges, placing them over the line just cut. (Use the strap hinges for the lower Dutch door and the oven door; use the butt hinges for the upper Dutch door and the remaining windows.) Finish cutting out the window or door, and you will see that it opens and closes perfectly.

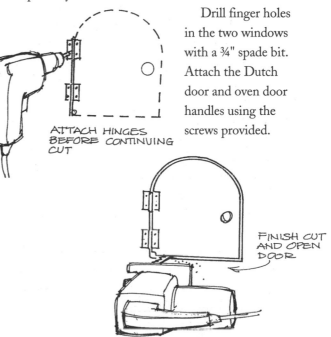

Drill finger holes in the two windows with a ¾" spade bit. Attach the Dutch door and oven door handles using the screws provided.

Step Four

Wall Assembly

After the windows and door are completed, nail the side walls to the front and rear walls, using 2½" siding nails every 4" to 6".

Step Five

Roof

Cut the 42"x48" main roof panels from the ⅜" exterior plywood. Attach them to the top edge of the front and rear walls, using 2½" siding nails every 6".

Step Six

Gable Dormer

This little dormer can be made from leftover scrap plywood. Cut the front of the dormer out of ¾" plywood according to the plans and cut out a 7"-wide opening. Notice the angled shape of the front: This will result in the sides being splayed. Cut the sides out of ⅜" plywood and nail them to the edges of the front of the dormer using 2½" siding nails.

GALVANIZED SIDING NAIL
USE THIS TO NAIL THE ⅜" PLYWOOD TO THE ¾" PLYWOOD

Cut the side walls and dormer roof to match the curve of the main roof. The best way to establish the correct curve is to hold the piece of ⅜" plywood up to the front or back edge of the roof and scribe a line with a pencil where the plywood meets the roof. Cut the plywood along this line with a jigsaw.

Use 1¼" deck screws to attach the dormer to the roof and screw them in at an angle, as you would when toenailing a nail.

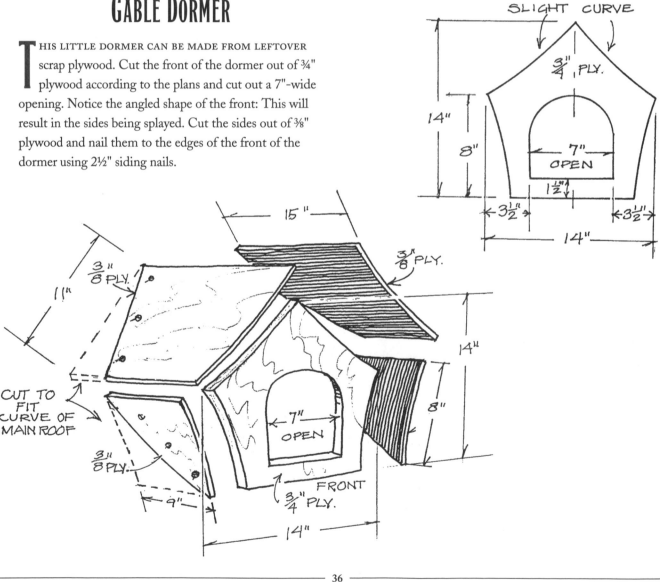

Step Seven

Shingles for Dormer & Main Roof

Using a jigsaw, cut ten 12"x48" strips from the ¼" plywood. Then, cut a scalloped edge on the bottom edge of each panel. Starting at the bottom, nail five strips to each side of the ⅜" plywood roof using 1" roofing nails, overlapping the top edge of each panel by 4". (After these are painted with white glossy enamel, they resemble icing on a cake.) Cut six 6"-wide panels for the gable dormer shingles and nail them on with 1" roofing nails.

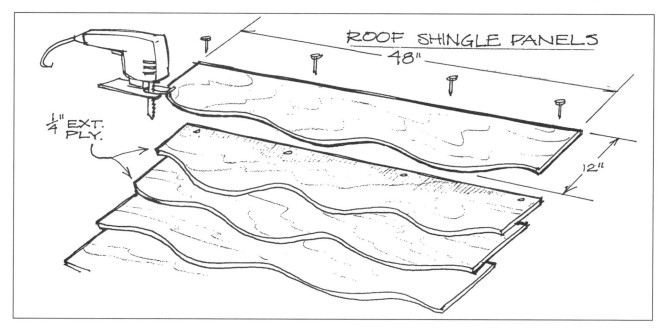

ROOF SHINGLE PANELS
48"

¼" EXT. PLY.

12"

Step Eight

Vergeboards

Cut twelve 2"x2" cedar blocks 6" long to make the support blocks. Drill two ⅛"-diameter pilot holes in each block and nail them to the underside of the eaves with 2½" siding nails, as shown in the illustration.

Using a jigsaw, cut the vergeboards out of ¼" plywood. Cut four strips 6"x42". Scallop the edges to resemble dripping icing on a cake, and attach the vergeboards to the blocks with 1¼" deck screws.

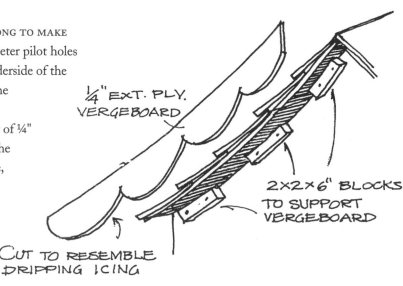

¼" EXT. PLY. VERGEBOARD

2×2×6" BLOCKS TO SUPPORT VERGEBOARD

CUT TO RESEMBLE DRIPPING ICING

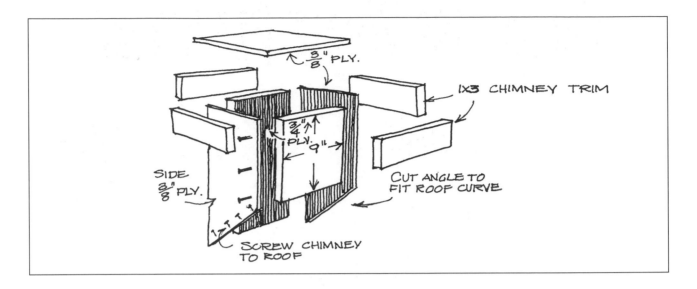

$\frac{3}{8}$" PLY.

1x3 CHIMNEY TRIM

$\frac{3}{4}$" PLY. 9"

CUT ANGLE TO FIT ROOF CURVE

SIDE $\frac{3}{8}$" PLY.

SCREW CHIMNEY TO ROOF

Step Nine

CHIMNEY

THE CHIMNEY IS CUT FROM LEFTOVER PIECES OF $\frac{3}{8}$" and $\frac{3}{4}$" plywood. As with the dormer, the bottom of the chimney must be cut to fit the curve of the roof, before it is screwed to the roof with 1¼" deck screws.

Step Ten

STOPS

IN ORDER TO PREVENT THE DOORS AND WINDOWS from swinging in too far, build stops. For the windows and the top Dutch door, screw a 1x3 onto the inside bottom of each opening using 1¼" deck screws. (Screw the 1x3 to the top of the lower Dutch door.) Position the stop so it is ½" higher than the bottom of the door or window opening. For the lower Dutch door, screw a 1x3 inside the door on the side opposite the hinges using 1¼" deck screws.

Step Eleven

DECORATIONS

CAKE AND CANDY DECORATIONS CAN BE CUT OUT OF plywood, or you can make realistic-looking cookies by rolling out a flat slab of clay and cutting out shapes with cookie cutters. If the playhouse is to be kept outside, the clay decorations must be fired in a kiln; otherwise, dry them in an oven, paint them with enamel and glue them onto the playhouse with non-toxic white glue.

Of course, if the playhouse is going to be inside, real cookies or play dough cookies can be used. This is where your kids can let their imaginations run wild. Gum drops, jelly beans, licorice, marshmallows and any other colorful candies can be glued on to create unique, individualized decorations.

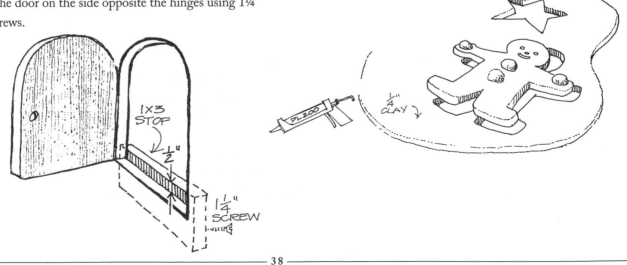

1x3 STOP

½"

1¼" SCREW

$\frac{1}{4}$" CLAY

PL200

FIBERGLASS WHALE PLAYHOUSE

I BUILT THIS UNIQUE PLAY STRUCTURE FOR
The Dalton School in New York City. Because the school's playground is on the roof, the space required a lightweight structure that could be safely climbed on by several kids at once. Originally, I designed an amorphous structure with slanting sides. As the various elements evolved and grew together, they assumed the shape of an animal with eyes and an open mouth. When it was finished, the kids nicknamed it the "whale."

Children of all ages have fun climbing the ropes hanging from the sides of the whale, and once they reach the top, they can peer down through a porthole at their playmates. They will never run out of games to play centered around the whale—everything from "king of the mountain," "ring around the whale" and "Moby Dick" to just playing "house" or "hide-and-seek."

The techniques for building this structure can be used to create almost any shape. There are unlimited possibilities as long as you are able to build an armature that can be covered with chicken wire, burlap and plaster. A project that in the beginning may appear complex actually goes rather quickly and is very gratifying.

MATERIALS				TOOLS
Quantity	Description	Size	Location	saw
3	½" CDX ply.	4'x8'	base	drop cloth
5	2x4 P.T. lumber	8'	base	hammer
4 pieces	¼"x1⅜" lattice	12'	frame	paper mixing buckets (for resin)
18 pieces	¼"x⅞" lattice	12'	frame	staple gun
1 spool	medium-gauge wire			sponges
50'	1"x1" chicken wire	24" high	covering	large scissors
100'	burlap roll	30" high	covering	disposable gloves
25 lbs.	plaster of paris		covering	clippers
2 bags	Structolite	80 lbs.	covering	six disposable 3" paint brushes
40 yds.	lightweight fiberglass cloth	38" high	covering	pliers
15 gals.	polyester resin & hardener		covering	rotary sander
small jar	white pigment			mixing bin (for plaster)
2 bags	thickening powder*			portable electric jigsaw
1	⅜"-thick Plexiglas	14" dia.	skylight	trowel
2	⅛"-thick Plexiglas dome	6" dia.	eyes	V.S.R. drill
	indoor/outdoor carpeting			¼" drill bit
	flooring adhesive			extension cord
50'	nylon rope	½"	climbing rope	
14	galv. eye bolts with	¼"x2"	rope fasteners	*Thickening powder
	washers & nuts			(Thixotropic powder) can be found
1 lb.	galv. finishing nails	6d		at most boatyards
1 gal.	acetone			

STEP ONE

BASE

CUT ONE SHEET OF PLYWOOD TO 6' LONG. FIND A level site and nail the three sheets of plywood together by placing pressure-treated 2x4s under the adjoining edges and nailing into them with 6d nails. (See below for the positioning of the plywood sheets.)

Cut the remaining pieces of 2x4s into blocks of various lengths for shims and slip them under the plywood to level the floor.

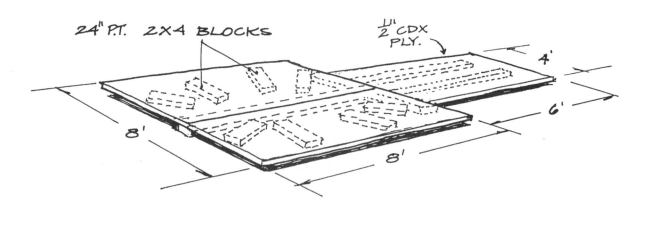

Step Two

Frame

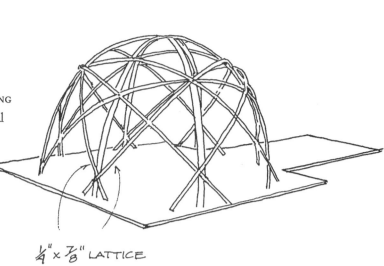

¼" × ⅞" LATTICE

Draw an 8'-diameter circle on the two abutting 4'x8' sheets of plywood and divide it into eight equal parts, marking them with a pencil. Make a slot at each point by drilling two ¼" holes 1⅜" apart and cutting out the plywood between them.

Take four pieces of 1⅜" lattice and bend the ends into the slots you have made.

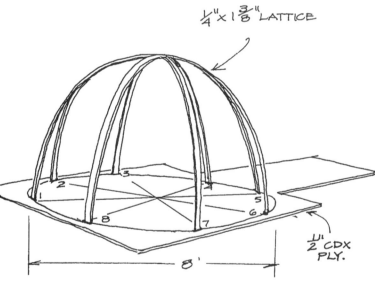

¼" × 1⅜" LATTICE

½" CDX PLY.

8'

Take eight pieces of ⅞" lattice and bend each one diagonally over the previous arches, weaving them over and under the existing lattice to form a dome. Connect the lattice where they intersect by boring a small hole through the lattice and tying each joint with wire.

Bend two more strips of ⅞" lattice to form a frame for each opening, toenailing the ends of the lattice to the plywood base using 6d nails (see A). Connect each door frame to the main

structure with three additional pieces of ⅞" lattice (see B). Bend shorter pieces of ⅞" lattice to form the arch of the tunnel that leads to the mouth opening, tying wire around the joints of the intersecting lattice (see C). Use ⅞" lattice as diagonal cross bracing wherever necessary, attaching it with wire where the lattice pieces intersect and nailing the ends to the base with 6d nails.

Cut away the plywood base to conform to the desired shape.

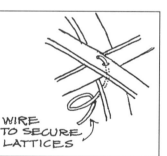

WIRE TO SECURE LATTICES

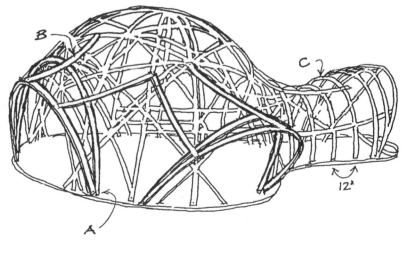

12"

STEP THREE
CHICKEN-WIRE COVERING

COVER THE ENTIRE STRUCTURE WITH 1"X 1" CHICKEN wire and staple it to the lattice frame. Wrap the chicken wire around each opening and under the base and fasten it securely.

STEP FOUR
BURLAP COVERING

SOAK THE BURLAP IN PLASTER OF PARIS AND, STARTING from the bottom and working up, completely cover the chicken wire with two layers of saturated burlap. The saturated cloth will strengthen the frame once it has set.

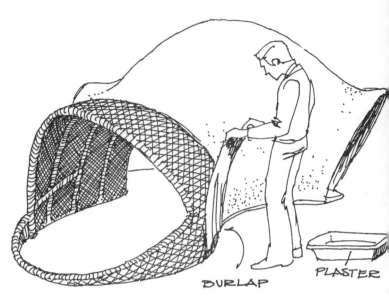

BURLAP PLASTER

STEP FIVE
STRUCTOLITE COVERING

TROWEL ON A ½" COAT OF STRUCTOLITE, using a sponge to sculpt a smooth surface.

STEP SIX
FIBERGLASS COVERING

ONCE THE STRUCTOLITE HAS THOROUGHLY DRIED (in approximately three days), cover the structure with two layers of fiberglass cloth saturated with polyester resin. Follow with three coats of resin mixed with white pigment and thickening powder. Resin cures very quickly (especially in warm weather), so mix small batches and work quickly!

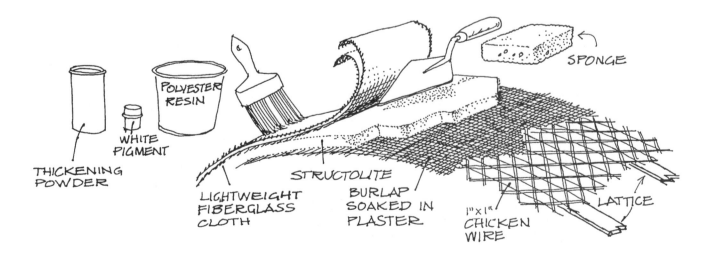

SPONGE

POLYESTER RESIN

WHITE PIGMENT

THICKENING POWDER

LIGHTWEIGHT FIBERGLASS CLOTH

STRUCTOLITE

BURLAP SOAKED IN PLASTER

1"X 1" CHICKEN WIRE

LATTICE

FIBERGLASSING TIPS

Fiberglass, as the name implies, is made of tiny strands of glass woven into different types of wool or cloth. Once it is saturated with either polyester resin and is "laid up" over some type of base form, it cures—usually within a few minutes—and forms a hard surface. Several layers of fiberglass are necessary to build up a shell ⅛" thick. A perfectly smooth surface can be made by filling in the dents and valleys with auto body filler and grinding down the ridges with a portable electric grinder.

◆ Never alter the proportions by adding more hardener (catalyst) to the mix. It will not set faster.

◆ Never work with fiberglass when the temperature is below 60 degrees F or above 80 degrees F.

◆ Wear a long-sleeved shirt and disposable gloves.

◆ Work in a well-ventilated area.

◆ Stir resin/hardener thoroughly for one minute before using.

◆ Mix only small quantities. Large batches heat up more quickly and give you less time to work.

◆ To make a thicker paste (to fill dents), use a thickening powder like Thixotropic powder.

◆ Use acetone to clean hands and tools.

FINAL TOUCHES

SKYLIGHT & EYE OPENINGS

Using a jigsaw, cut out a 14"-diameter opening for the skylight, making a beveled cut as if you were cutting the top of a jack-o'-lantern. Lay the 14"-diameter flat piece of

SKYLIGHT

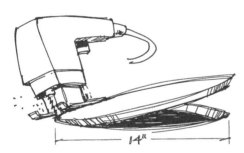

Plexiglas on top of the cutout and seal the edges with polyester resin that has been made into a stiff paste with thickening powder. Provide two "eye" windows by cutting out two 6"-diameter holes and attaching the Plexiglas domes as shown.

INTERIOR

Plaster the interior with a ½" coat of Structolite, and paint it (not a job for someone with a bad back!) after it has dried.

FLOORING

To protect hands and knees from scrapes and bruises, cut a roll of indoor/outdoor carpeting to fit the floor space inside the whale and glue it to the plywood base with flooring adhesive.

CLIMBING ROPES

Drill ¼" holes for the eye bolts in strategic locations. Insert the bolts through the structure and secure them on the inside of the whale with a washer and nut. For protection, coat the bolts, washers and nuts with thickened polyester resin after they have been secured. Attach ropes to the eye bolts to help climbers reach the top of the whale.

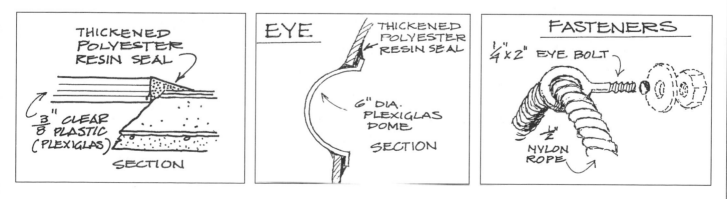

Barn Bed Playhouse

AGE RANGE 5 TO 12

THIS PLAYHOUSE IS ACTUALLY A BED DESIGNED to look like a barn. It's especially nice for city kids who wish they lived in the country. The wall next to the bed can be decorated or painted with a farm or ranch scene, and a "fake" window can be built into the bed with a pastoral scene painted inside the window frame.

This playhouse is a great way to provide extra storage in a room while also providing a special, private place for your child. These instructions are for a standard twin mattress that is 39"x80"x8" high.

MATERIALS

Quantity	Description	Size	Location
2	4x4 cedar posts	10'	corner posts
4	2x6 #2 fir	8'	side supports
2	2x6 #2 fir	10'	crossties
1	4x4 cedar post	8'	diagonal braces
1	¾"-dia. wood dowel	2'	diagonal brace pegs
1	2x4 #2 fir	8'	rails
5	1x3 #2 pine	8'	cross braces, headboard window trim, gable trim
2	2x2 #2 cedar	10'	bed-board support (side & end)
1	⅝" ply.	4'x8'	bed board
3	⅝" text. 1-11 ply. (grooves every 4")	4'x8'	end-wall panels, roof
1	1x2 #2 pine	8'	hayloft window trim
1	⅛"-thick Plexiglas	13"x13"	headboard window
1	1x8 #2 pine	8'	shelves
	carpenter's glue		
1 pair	hinges	1½"x1½"	hayloft window
1	knob		hayloft window
8	galv. sheet metal screws	½"	
36	galv. lag screws	⅜"x4"	
1 box	galv. drywall screws	1½"	
1 box	galv. drywall screws	2½"	
1 box	galv. finishing nails	4d	

TOOLS

tape measure
hammer
pencil
framing square
speed square
level
sandpaper
chalk line
vice grip pliers
V.S.R. drill
Phillips head screwdriver bit
¼", ½" & ¾" spade drill bits
portable electric circular saw
extension cord
magic markers

STEP ONE

FRAMING THE BED

CUT A 10' 4X4 POST INTO TWO PIECES, EACH ONE measuring 59½" long. Do the same with the other 10' 4x4 post. Lay two of the posts on the floor, parallel to each other, and 80" apart (measuring outside edge to outside edge).

For the side supports, cut the four 8' 2x6s into 80" lengths. Lay one of these across the posts, placing it 14" up from the bottom of the posts. Using 2½" screws, screw the 2x6 to the 4x4 posts.

Turn the posts over and screw another 80" 2x6 to the top of the posts, using two ⅜"x4" lag screws at each end. Repeat the same steps for the second set of 4x4 posts.

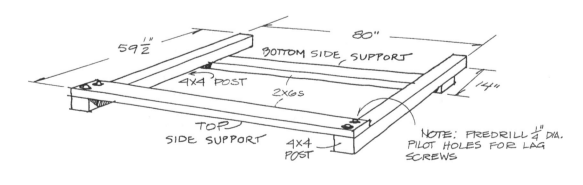

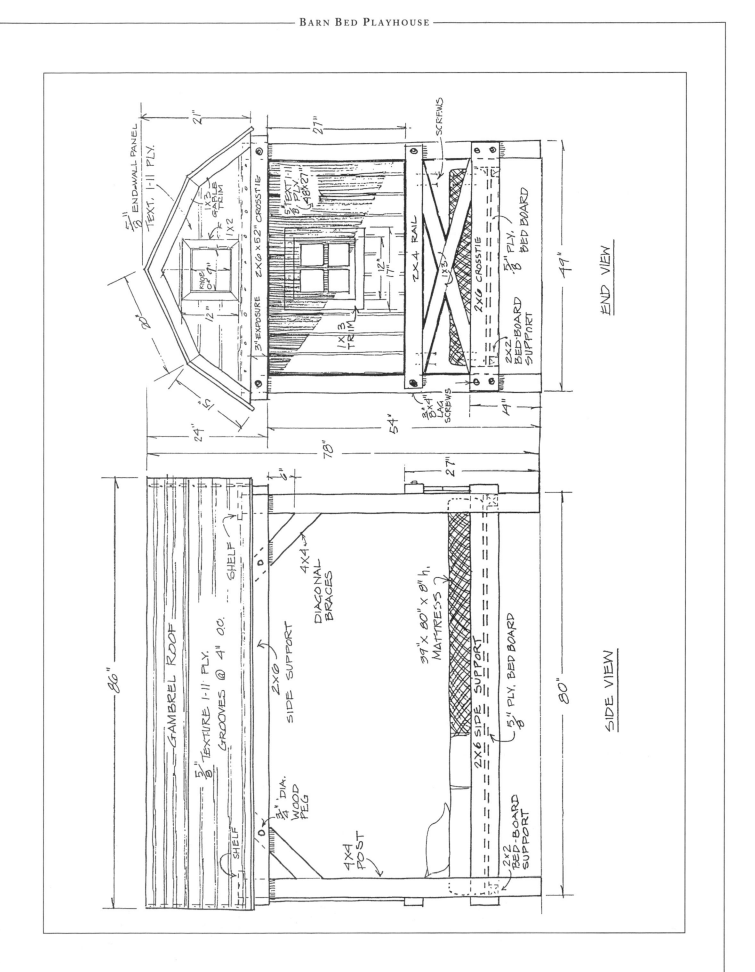

END VIEW

SIDE VIEW

To make the crossties, cut a 10' 2x6 into two 49"-long pieces. Stand one set of posts up against a wall and use the lag screws to screw the 2x6 to the outside of the post, 14" up from the bottom. Have an assistant stand up the second set of posts and screw the other end of the 2x6 crosstie to this set of posts. Repeat these steps on the other end of the bed.

Cut the remaining 10' 2x6 into two pieces, both 52" long. Attach these crossties to the top ends of the sets of posts.

To make the diagonal braces for the bed posts, cut the 8' 4x4 post into four pieces, each 24" long. Then cut each end off at a 45-degree angle. Using the Phillips head bit, screw the bottom of each brace to the 4x4 bed post with 2½" drywall screws. Join the top of the brace to the 2x6 side support by drilling a ¾"-diameter hole with a ¾" spade drill bit through the side support and into the side of the brace. Pound a ¾" peg into the hole.

RAILS & CROSS BRACES

CUT THE 8' 2X4 INTO TWO PIECES EACH MEASURING 4' long. Screw these rails into the 4x4 posts at each end of the bed using lag screws, so that the top of each rail is 27" from the floor.

Cut four 4'-long 1x3 cross braces for both ends of the bed. Chisel out a notch in both braces where they cross in the center. Join the cross braces to the 2x6 crosstie and the 2x4 rails with 2½" screws.

BED BOARD

TO SUPPORT THE BED BOARD, CUT EACH 2X2 TO measure 77" for the side bed-board supports. Cut the leftover 2x2s to measure 39" each for the end bed-board supports. Screw each piece to the bottom inside edge of the bed frame (the lower side supports and the lower crossties) using 2½" screws every 6".

To make the bed board, cut the ⅝" piece of plywood to measure 39"x80" and, using 1½" drywall screws, attach it to the 2x2 bed-board support.

STEP FOUR
END-WALL PANELS & WINDOWS

CUT THE PANELS FOR THE HEADBOARD AND THE TWO gable ends out of one sheet of ⅝" texture plywood, cutting the panels to the dimensions shown in the end-view plan (see page 47). Cut the 12"x12" headboard

window opening out of the largest of the three panels and frame it with 1x3s. Cut the hayloft window out of the gable panel for the foot of the bed and frame it with 1x2s. Attach the panel just cut out with 1½"x1½" hinges and attach the knob to the outside of this "door." Nail the three end-wall panels in place every 6" using 4d finishing nails.

To make your barn bed playhouse really authentic, use transparent dyes, such as magic markers, and paint a farm scene and window muntins on a piece of translucent Plexiglas. Screw the Plexiglas behind the headboard window opening with sheet metal screws and shine a light through from the other side. A bucolic farm scene with "sunlight" filtering through will make a great view, framed by gingham curtains.

STEP FIVE
ROOF

CUT TWO 15"x86" PANELS AND TWO 20"x86" PANELS from the ⅝" plywood. Position the roof panels so they overhang the end-wall panels by 1½", then glue and screw them using 1½" drywall screws to the top edge of the end-wall panels. Cut the 1x3 gable trim according to the specifications in the end-view plan and nail it in place with 4d finishing nails.

STEP SIX
SHELVES

CUT THE 1x8 #2 PINE INTO TWO 48"-LONG PIECES AND screw them to the tops of the 4x4 posts with 1½" drywall screws. This will provide a shelf at each end of the bed.

THREE-LEGGED FORT

I DESIGNED AND BUILT THIS FORT AS A "demo" in several shopping malls across the United States in order to promote owner-built play structures. Part of its popularity is that it can be constructed in one afternoon at a minimal cost. Its final resting place was the roof of the 92nd Street YMCA Nursery School in New York City, where kids are still climbing on it, searching for horizons through the skyscrapers.

The stairway is an optional feature that can be replaced by a simple wooden ladder or even a rope ladder. It has been our experience, however, that the more accessible the playhouse, the more it is used. When your children outgrow this fort, the bottom can be enclosed to transform it into a pool pump/filter enclosure or even a bell tower.

MATERIALS

Quantity	Description	Size	Location
3	2x8 fir beams	10'	floor beams, roof beams
3	6"-dia. P.T. posts	8'	corner posts
1	1x2 #2 pine	10'	floor support
2	⅝" ext. ply.	4'x8'	floor, roof
1	2x4 #2 fir	8'	door post
3	2x4 #2 fir	10'	railings
6	1x4 #2 pine	8'	railing slats
1	2x6 #2 fir	10'	stair legs
1	2x6 #2 fir	8'	stair treads
2	2x4 #2 fir	8'	stair rails, railing posts
1	1x4 #2 pine	8'	support cleats
26	galv. lag screws & washers	½"x4"	
16	galv. lag screws & washers	⅜"x4"	
8	galv. carriage bolts	⅜"x3½"	
1 lb.	galv. finishing nails	8d	
1 box	galv. deck screws	2"	

TOOLS

tape measure
level
speed square
chalk line
V.S.R. drill
½" & ⅜" spade drill bits
vise grip pliers
hammer
portable electric circular saw
portable electric jigsaw
stepladder
chisel
utility knife
extension cord

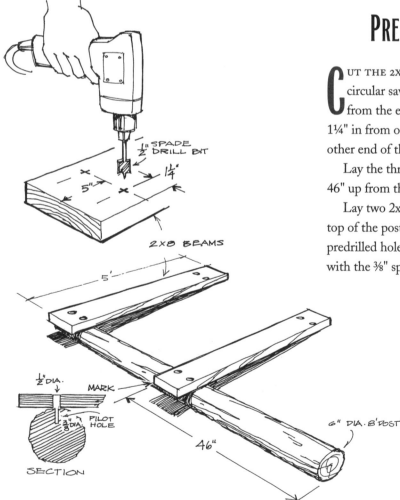

STEP ONE

PREPARING BEAMS & POSTS

CUT THE 2X8 BEAMS INTO SIX 5' LENGTHS WITH A circular saw. Drill two holes with the ½" spade bit 5" from the end of each beam. Each hole should each be 1¼" in from one side of the beam. Repeat the same on the other end of the beam.

Lay the three round 8' posts on the ground and mark 46" up from the bottom of each one.

Lay two 2x8 beams over one of the posts: one at the top of the post and one at the 46" mark. Using the predrilled holes in the beams as a guide, drill pilot holes with the ⅜" spade bit, 2" deep, into the center of the posts.

Step Two

Attaching Beams & Posts

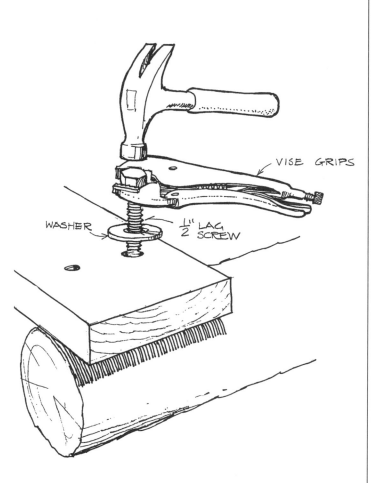

VISE GRIPS

WASHER

$\frac{1}{2}$" LAG SCREW

Lock a pair of vise grip pliers onto the head of a ½" lag screw, so that the head protrudes above the pliers by ⅛". Attach a washer to the lag screw and start it into one of the holes in the beam by giving the head of the screw a few hard taps with a hammer. Turn the lag screw one revolution at a time between sharp blows with the hammer. After several revolutions, the threads of the screw will catch the wood and hammering will no longer be necessary. Screw the lag screw all the way into the beam until you see that the washer is beginning to depress the wood. Do the same for the other hole in the beam, and repeat the entire procedure for the other two posts. You now have three sets of posts with two beams secured to each one.

Step Three

Floor Support

Turn the post over so that the back sides of the beams are facing up (see illustration below). Cut and nail a 40" long 1x2 floor support ¾" below the top edge of the lower beam and 10" in from the end. Repeat for the other two posts.

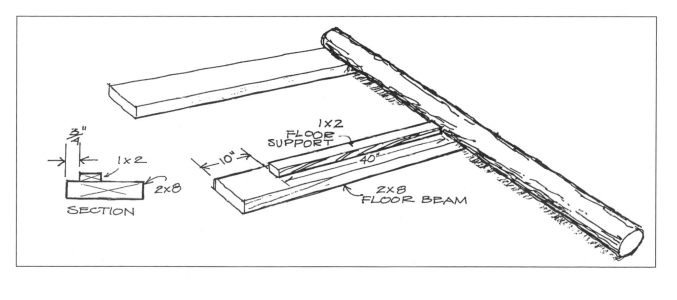

$\frac{3}{4}$"

1x2

2x8

SECTION

1x2 FLOOR SUPPORT

10"

40"

2x8 FLOOR BEAM

STEP FOUR
FLOOR & ROOF

TO MAKE THE FLOOR AND ROOF PANELS, MARK AND cut the two sheets of ⅝" plywood according to the plan below, using a circular saw.

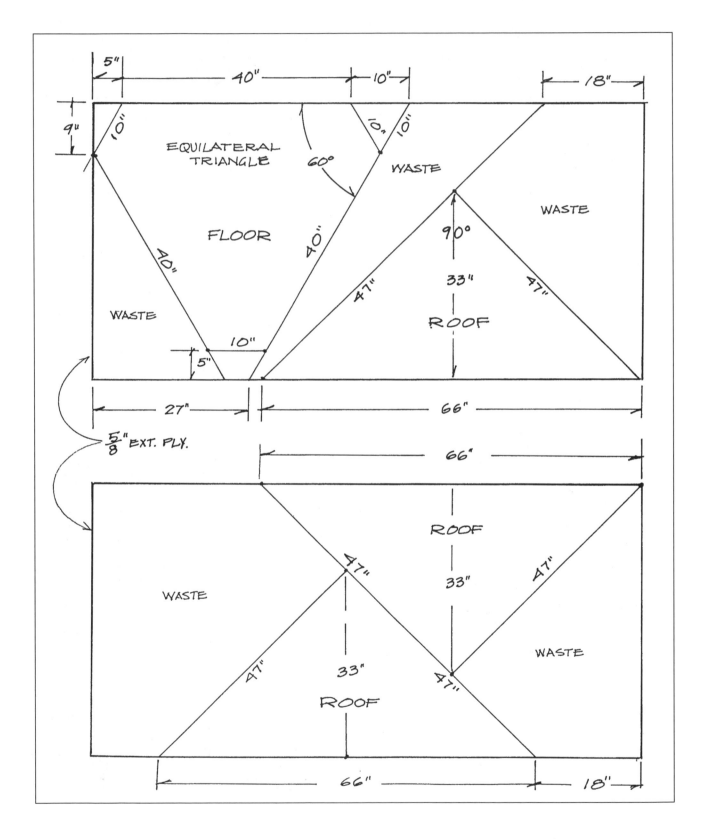

STEP FIVE
ASSEMBLY

WITH THE HELP OF TWO ASSISTANTS, STAND THE three posts up and insert the floor board, temporarily nailing it in place. It should rest on top of the 1x2, almost flush with the top of the lower beams.

To secure the unfastened end of each 2x8 floor beam, drill two ⅜"-diameter pilot holes in each post 46" up from the ground (as in Step One). Screw the ½" lag screws through the holes in the end of the predrilled beams into the posts (as in Step Two). Once the lower screws are in place, stand on a stepladder and drill pilot holes into the top of the posts (using the predrilled beam holes as a guide). Bolt the roof beams to the posts with lag screws.

STEP SIX
DOOR POST & RAILINGS

TO MAKE THE DOOR POST, CUT THE 8' 2X4 TO MEASURE 57½" long using a jigsaw, and cut 1½"x3½" notches in the 2x4 in the locations shown in the plan. Drill two ⅜"-diameter holes in the top and bottom of the post. Measure and mark 30 " from the outside edge of the 2x8 roof and floor beams. Line up the stair-side face of the door post with the marks. Screw the door post to the upper and lower beams, using ⅜"x4" lag screws.

To construct the railings on the stair side, cut two pieces of 2x4, each 30" long, and screw them into the door post notches and the left corner post with ⅜"x4" lag screws. For the other two sides, cut four more 2x4s, each 5' long, and screw them to the outside of the remaining two posts with ⅜"x4" lag screws so that the top edges of the railings measure 6" and 22" from the floor.

Nail 1x4 railing slats spaced 1" apart to the inside of the playhouse railing. Allow the slats to protrude at least 1" above the top edge of the railing. Sand the top edges to round off the sharp corners.

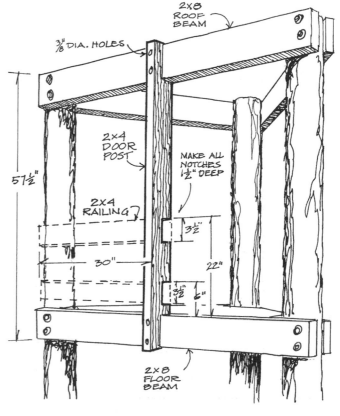

STEP SEVEN

ROOF

WITH AN ASSISTANT, ASSEMBLE THE THREE PLYWOOD roof panels on the ground and secure them together with 8d finishing nails spaced 6" apart. Then lift the roof onto the beams and secure them with 2" deck screws every 6".

STEP EIGHT

STAIRS

BUILD THE STAIRS AS DESCRIBED IN "LADDER" ON PAGE 85. For an extra-safe stairway, add a 2x4 railing. Cut the railings and posts out of 2x4s and, using ⅜"x3½" carriage bolts, bolt the stair railings to the railing posts. Then, use ½"x4" lag screws to screw the top of the stair railings to the door post and the corner post.

STEP NINE

WIND ORNAMENT

YOU CAN MAKE AN EFFECTIVE WIND ORNAMENT, very simply, out of a used plastic bottle. A Clorox bottle is the perfect size. Using a utility knife, cut three flaps and fold them out. Cut a broom handle to your desired length and push it through the neck of the plastic bottle. Secure it to the other end of the bottle with a small nail. (In order to allow the ornament to turn more easily, you will need to make the hole for the nail in the Clorox bottle slightly bigger than the nail you are using. This is easily done by first hammering a bigger nail in the hole and then removing it.) Nail a triangular piece of plywood to the ceiling of the roof at the peak. Drill a hole the same size as the diameter of the broom handle through the roof and the plywood triangle and tap the broom handle through these holes to hold the wind ornament in place. You will be amazed at how little wind it takes to make the ornament turn. If your kids decide to replace the ornament with a flag, it will make a great gadget to keep moles out of your garden!

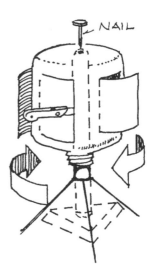

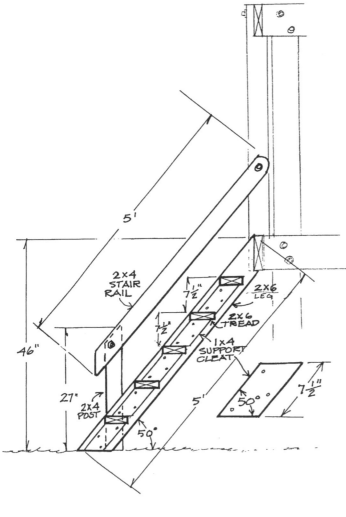

TRADITIONAL PLAYHOUSE

AGE
RANGE
7 TO 11

THIS IS AN EXCELLENT PROJECT FOR A parent or grandparent who has some time on his or her hands and has had experience working with hand and power tools. The playhouse is 6'x6', so it is small enough to be prefabricated in the basement and then moved in sections to the final site.

The windows are the most difficult part of this playhouse. I have described how they can be made using a table saw (see p. 15); however, you may want to simplify things by special-ordering them from your lumberyard. The shutters can also be bought, pre-made, from catalogs and building supply stores, and the fancy scrolls can be ordered through the mail as well. The front door features a heart-shaped window through which your child can peek out at visitors with love.

This is a great playhouse in which kids can practice their interior-decorating skills. For more sophisticated house dwellers, battery-operated lights and a cordless telephone can be kept inside. For down-home folks, a flashlight and a walkie-talkie can be just as much fun. Thrift-shop furniture or packing crates can be decorated and arranged artfully, and curtains can be easily hung by clipping fabric remnants or tea towels to a curtain rod. This is a luxurious way for kids to camp out in their "own" home away from home.

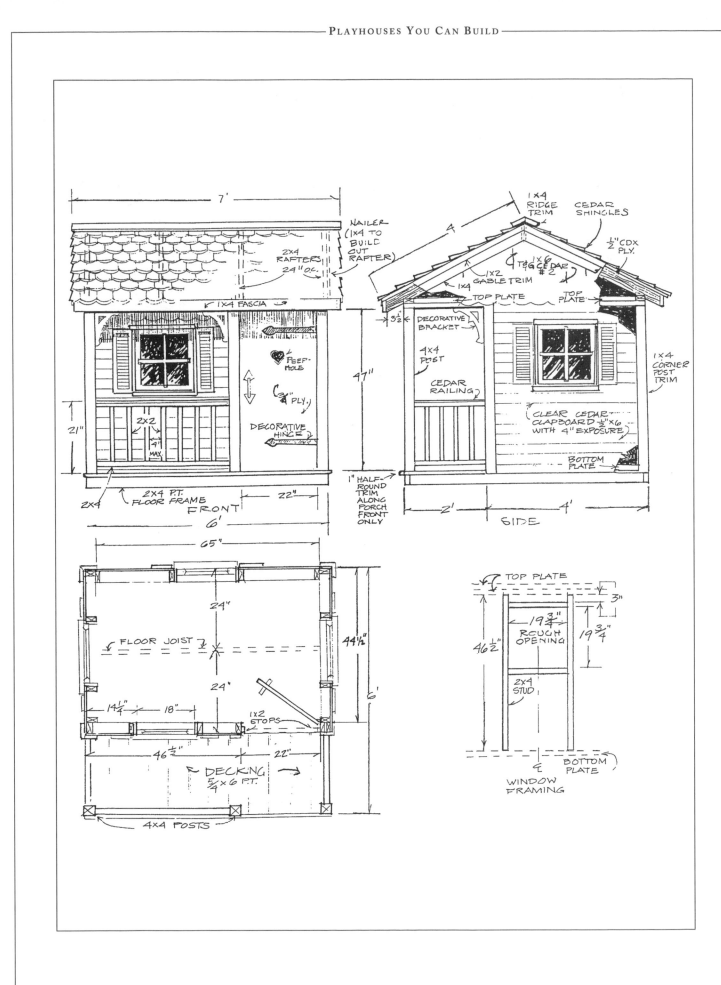

MATERIALS

Quantity	Description	Size	Location
2	solid concrete blocks	8"x16"x4"	corners
3	2x4 P.T. lumber	12'	floor frame, floor joists
1	¾" A/D ply.	4'x8'	interior floor, door
2	5/4x6 P.T. lumber	12'	exterior decking
1	1" half-round molding	6'	deck edging
2	4x4 fir posts	8'	porch posts
16	2x4 #2 fir	8'	wall studs, side wall bottom plates, roof rafters, bottom porch railing
6	2x4 #2 fir	12'	top plates, front wall bottom plate, back wall bottom plate
2	½" CDX ply.	4'x8'	roof, gusset plates
12	1x4 #2 pine	8'	ridgepole, gable ends (nailer), corner post trim, door trim, gable trim, roof ridge trim
205 lin. ft.	clapboard	½"x6	wall siding
4	1x6 #2 cedar T&G	10'	gables
1	1x4 #2 pine	14'	fascia boards
4	1x2 #2 pine	8'	gable trim, door stop
3 boxes	round-bottom fancy-cut cedar shingles	3" wide	roof
4	2x2 clear cedar	8'	balusters
1	cedar railing	8'	porch
1 pair	galv. hinges	1½"x3"	door
2	handles	5"	door
1 pair	decorative black strap hinges		door
4	windows with 4 lights	18"x18"	walls
8	decorative shutters	6"x18"	windows
4	decorative brackets		porch
1 gal.	paint		

TOOLS

shovel
tape measure
level
framing square
speed square
chalk line
nail set
block plane
hammer
sandpaper
caulking gun
protractor
V.S.R. drill
Phillips head screwdriver bit
extension cord
portable electric jigsaw
portable electric circular saw
paint brush

NAILS, ETC.

1 lb.	6d galv. common nails
2 lbs.	20d galv. common nails
3 lbs.	10d galv. common nails
3 lbs.	3d galv. shingling nails
3 lbs.	6d galv. siding nails
1 lb.	8d galv. finishing nails

NOTE:

It's best to use pressure-treated lumber wherever lumber is in contact with the ground. But because it is treated with chemicals, pressure-treated lumber should only be used as a base for the playhouse. It should not be sanded, and it is best to wear gloves when working with it.

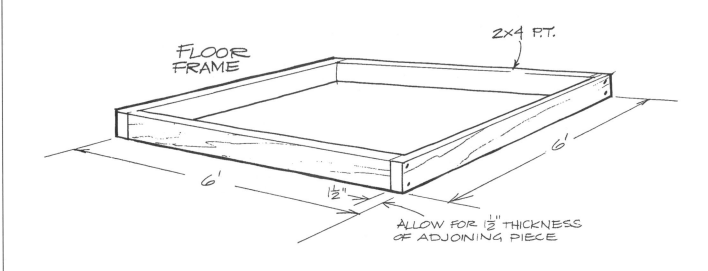

FLOOR FRAME

2x4 P.T.

6'

6'

1½"

ALLOW FOR 1½" THICKNESS OF ADJOINING PIECE

STEP ONE

BASE

BEGIN BY CLEARING THE AREA WHERE YOU WANT the playhouse to go. To keep an eye on the kids, the playhouse should be located near the main house and within calling distance.

Build a 6'x6' frame for the floor by cutting pressure-treated 2x4s with a circular saw and nailing them together with 10d nails. Remember to allow 1½" for the thickness of the adjoining piece.

Carefully mark and cut two 69" 2x4 floor joists and, using 20d common nails, nail them at 24" centers. Cut a

piece of ¾" A/D plywood to measure 4'x6'. Lay the plywood on top of the floor frame, using the plywood as a guide to check that the corners of the floor frame are square. Using 6d siding nails, nail the plywood to the floor frame and joists.

Next, nail the pressure-treated 5/4x6 decking to the porch floor frame, positioning it perpendicular to the front wall of the playhouse. Trim the front edge of the decking with half-round molding and nail it in place with 6d siding nails.

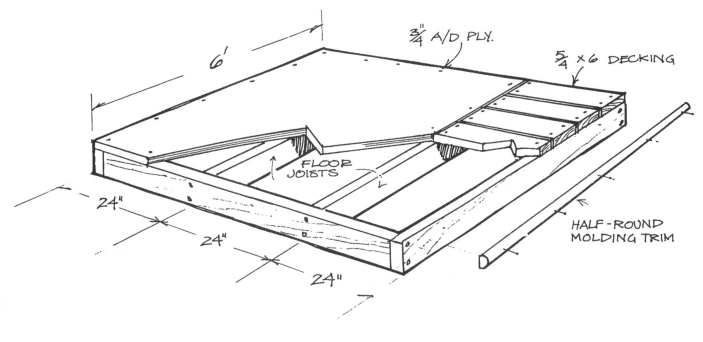

6'

¾" A/D PLY.

5/4 X6 DECKING

FLOOR JOISTS

24"

24"

24"

HALF-ROUND MOLDING TRIM

LEVELING THE FLOOR

Building sites are practically never level. An easy way to level the base of this one is to place 8"x16"x4" solid concrete blocks under the low end. Make sure the blocks rest on compacted soil and that the whole floor is absolutely level, since this will affect all subsequent construction on the playhouse.

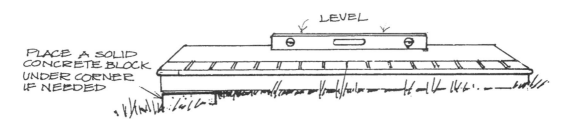

LEVEL

PLACE A SOLID CONCRETE BLOCK UNDER CORNER IF NEEDED

STEP TWO

FRAMING

CUT THE TWO 8' 4X4 FIR POSTS INTO FOUR 47" LENGTHS. Toenail three of them to the decking using 8d finishing nails. Following the plans on page 58, use 2x4s to construct each of the four walls separately, working on the floor of the playhouse, which serves as a level work space.

Use a temporary prop to hold the first wall in place while you nail the single-layer bottom plate to the floor of the playhouse with 10d common nails. Note that the porch does not have a bottom plate. After each wall is completed, tilt it into place and nail it to the adjoining wall using 10d common nails before building the next wall.

After the walls are complete, nail the bottom layer of top plate into the porch posts and toenail it into the bottom layer of the wall top plate using 10d nails. Do not nail on the second layer of the top plate until all four sides and the bottom layer of the top plate over the porch are in place. It is important that the joints of the top layer of the top plate do not line up with the joints of the bottom layer of the top plate (see detail).

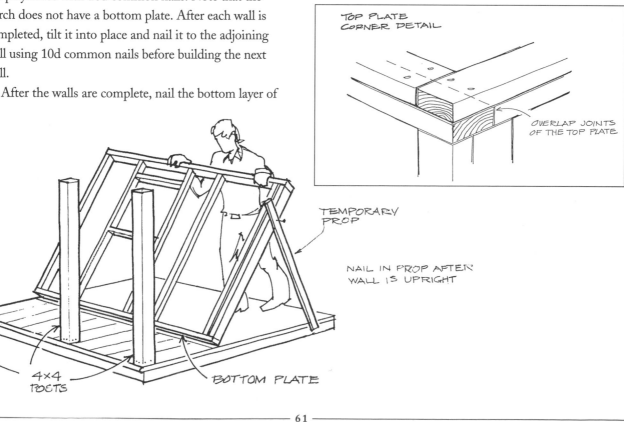

TOP PLATE CORNER DETAIL

OVERLAP JOINTS OF THE TOP PLATE

TEMPORARY PROP

NAIL IN PROP AFTER WALL IS UPRIGHT

4X4 POSTS

BOTTOM PLATE

STEP THREE
RAFTERS

To make the roof rafters, cut four of the 8' 2x4s in half. Using a protractor, mark a 26½-degree angle on both ends of the 4' rafters and cut off the ends at this angle. Make a 1½"x2" notch 4" from the bottom end of each rafter. This notch allows the bottom of the rafter to rest securely on top of the top plate.

Cut both of the CDX plywood panels to measure 4'x7' for the roof and set aside. With the leftover plywood, cut eight notched gusset plates as shown in the illustration.

To join the top ends of the rafters (still using the floor as a work platform), nail a gusset plate to each side of the rafters, leaving a ¾" space for the 1x4 ridgepole. Lift the pairs of rafters into position (at 24" centers) and slip the 7' ridgepole into the rafter notches. Toenail the bottom of the rafters to the top plates using 6d common nails. Check to make sure the rafters are plumb, then toenail the top of the rafters to the ridgepole.

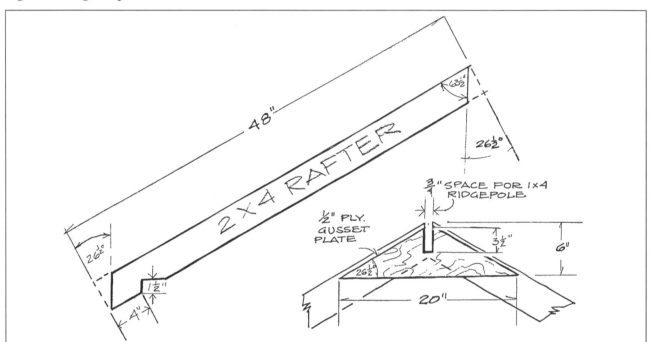

STEP FOUR
ROOF & SIDING

Nail the already-cut CDX plywood roof panels to the roof rafters using 6d common nails spaced 6" on-center.

Then, cut to fit and nail ½"x6 clear cedar clapboards onto the walls of the playhouse, using 6d siding nails. Overlap the boards so that 4" of each board is exposed. Finish off the ends of the siding by nailing the 1x4 corner post trim to the outside edges of the four corners with 6d siding nails.

STEP FIVE
GABLE ENDS & TRIM

To make the tongue & groove overlap the cedar clapboards, nail two pieces of 1x4 to the outside face of each end rafter. (This 1x4 is called a nailer.) Cut the tongue & groove to fit the space in the gable ends. Then, nail the cut pieces to the nailer and the top plate using 8d finishing nails. For a more decorative effect, round off the bottoms of the boards with a jigsaw. (Make a cardboard pattern and trace it onto the boards before cutting them.) Then, hold the 1x4 gable trim underneath the roof panels and nail through the roof into the 1x4 gable trim using 8d finishing nails (see illustration on facing page).

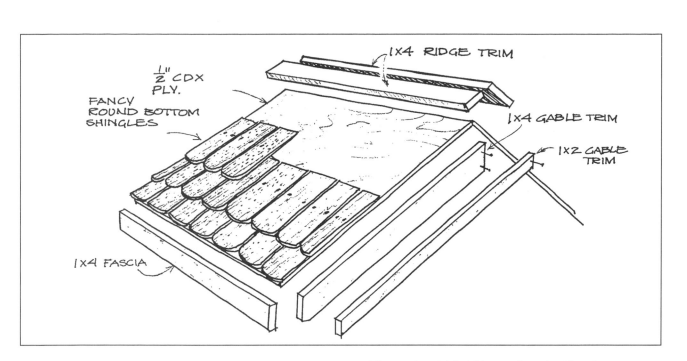

1" CDX PLY. (½")

FANCY ROUND BOTTOM SHINGLES

1X4 RIDGE TRIM

1X4 GABLE TRIM

1X2 GABLE TRIM

1X4 FASCIA

STEP SIX

FASCIA BOARDS & SHINGLES

FOR THE FASCIA BOARDS, CUT THE 14' 1X4 IN HALF AND nail these boards to the front and rear eaves of the roof. Then, nail 1x2 gable trim to the 1x4 gable trim. Shingling instructions are given on the package containing the shingles, but use 3d shingling nails even if other nails are specified to make sure the shingling nails do not protrude though the plywood panel into the interior. After all the shingles have been nailed on, nail the 1x4 ridge trim to the peak using 8d finishing nails.

STEP SEVEN

PORCH

FOR THE BOTTOM RAILING, CUT AN 8' 2X4 TO FIT between the porch posts (along the front) and between the post and the wall (along the sides). Then cut five balusters of equal length from each 8' 2x2. Space seven balusters equally between the porch posts and mark their locations on the 2x4. Then, position the balusters along the marks and nail through the 2x4 bottom railing into the end of the 2x2 balusters with 8d finishing nails. After all the balusters have been nailed onto the 2x4, toenail this assembly to the two posts, leaving a 2" space between the decking and the 2x4 bottom railing.

Then, using 8d finishing nails and nailing from underneath the railing, toenail the balusters to the cedar railing and this top railing to the posts.

Do the same for the side railings, using four balusters on each side, and toenailing one end to the porch post, and the other to the front wall.

STEP EIGHT

DOOR

THE DOOR IS MADE FROM THE LEFTOVER PIECE OF ¾" plywood that was used for the floor. Cut it to fit the opening and cut a heart-shaped peephole in the center. Notice that the door swings inward, which means that the hinges must be mounted on the inside of the playhouse.

Provide a stop for the door by nailing a 1x2 to each side and along the top of the door frame. Attach a handle to both the inside and outside of the door. For decoration, attach two fake strap hinges to the front of the door. Nail on the 1x4 door trim with 8d finishing nails.

STEP NINE

WINDOWS, SHUTTERS & BRACKETS

REFER TO SECTION ONE (P. 15) FOR WINDOW INSTRUCTIONS. Attach the decorative shutters and brackets according to the manufacturer's instructions.

SPOOK PLAYHOUSE

AGE RANGE 6 TO 10

MY DAUGHTER DISCOVERED THIS HAUNTED house at the Round Swamp Farm in East Hampton, New York, nestled between the farm stand and a wheelbarrow of chrysanthemums. A small witch sat at the front door, daring people to peek through the door crack. Skeletons hung from the ceiling, and luminous skulls and pumpkins all glowed against the black interior. A bat hovered in the corner, while a larger-than-life black widow dangled dangerously from one of the many spider webs crisscrossing the ceiling. Stocking caps covered monster heads made from innocent gourds and melons, and a glance to one side revealed a coffin complete with an unidentifiable Halloween monster. A witch's brew, foaming from a cauldron, looked extremely authentic, and a recording of scary Halloween sounds played when the door was opened farther. The outside of the house was a mottled gray, and fake shingles were painted on with dark accents, giving the exterior a weathered, decayed look. Tombstones made out of scrap plywood stood to the side. This was the ultimate haunted house. As you build your own, feel free to depart from the plans described here, but remember—the creepier, the better!

MATERIALS

Quantity	Description	Size	Location
1	2x6 P.T. lumber	8'	base
1	2x6 P.T. lumber	12'	base
3	¾" CDX ply.	4'x8'	floor, dormer, vergeboards, front wall, back wall
4	½" CDX ply.	4'x8'	side walls, dormer, roof
3	1x4 #2 pine	8'	roof ridge, window roof, window batten, door roof
2	1x3 #2 pine	10'	door frame, window frame, door stop
	construction adhesive		
	latex or enamel paint		fake windows, fake wood-grain walls
1	black handle	5"	door
1	knocker		door
1 pair	butt hinges	2½"x 3"	door
2 lbs.	galv. siding nails	2"	
1 lb.	galv. common nails	8d	
12	galv. common nails	10d	
24	finishing nails	3d	
1 box	galv. deck screws	1½"	

TOOLS

tape measure
level
hammer
speed square
framing square
rasp
chalk line
portable electric circular saw
portable electric jigsaw
V.S.R. drill
Phillips head screwdriver bit
extension cord
caulking gun
paint brush

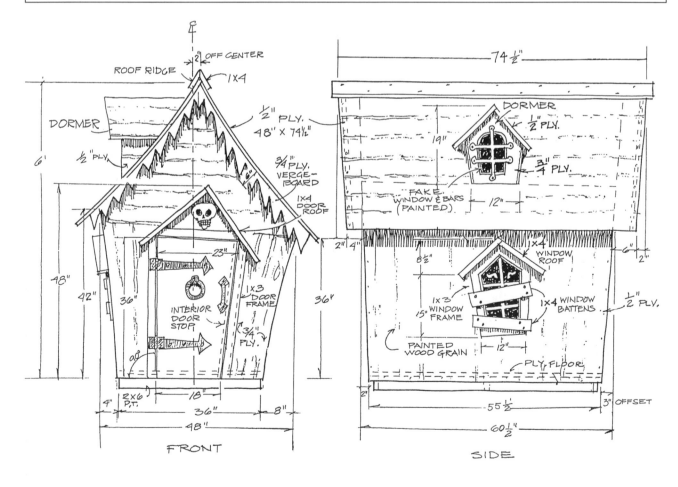

FRONT

SIDE

STEP ONE
BASE

SELECT A SITE THAT IS LEVEL AND REMOVE ANY ROOTS or rocks. Cut the 8' 2x6 into a 36" and a 51" piece. Then, cut the 12' 2x6 into a 36", a 51" and a 33" piece. To form the base frame, nail the lengths together according to the plan using 10d nails, centering the 33" middle support between the two 36" sides. Cut one of the sheets of ¾" CDX plywood to measure 36"x54" and nail this to the top of the base frame using 8d common nails.

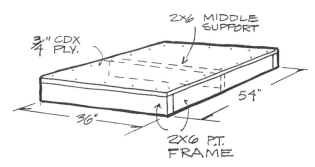

STEP TWO
WALLS & ROOF

CUT THE FRONT AND BACK WALLS OUT OF ¾" CDX plywood according to the plan. Do not cut the opening for the door yet. Cut the sides and the roof out of ½" CDX plywood (according to the plan) and glue and nail the side panels to the front and back panels, using construction adhesive and 2" siding nails.

Then, bend the roof panels to meet the curve of the front and rear panels. Glue and nail the roof panels to the walls using 2" siding nails. To form the roof ridge, nail two 1x4s to the peak of the roof with 8d nails.

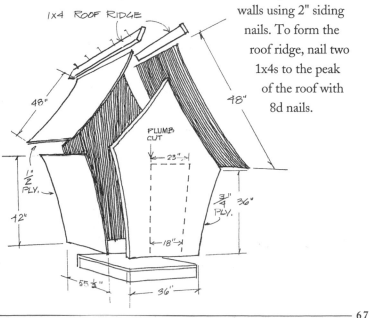

STEP THREE
DOOR & FAKE WINDOW

USING A JIGSAW, CUT OUT THE DOOR. CUT THE RIGHT side at an angle as shown, but make sure that the side with the hinges is cut plumb. Frame the door with 1x3s and hang the door using 2½"x3" butt hinges. (You can make strap hinges look medieval by cutting straps out of scrap ⅛" hardboard, painting them black, and gluing them to the front door.) Then attach the handle and the knocker.

To make the door stop, glue and nail a 1x3 to the side of the door opposite the hinges using 3d finishing nails.

Paint a fake window and muntins, then frame the "window" with 1x3s. Nail on 1x4 window battens using 3d finishing nails.

To install two 1x4 boards over the door (see plan, facing page), ask an assistant to hold them in place (on edge over the door), while you nail into them from inside the house. Use the same procedure for nailing on the window roof.

STEP FOUR
VERGEBOARDS

THE VERGEBOARDS ARE CUT FROM LEFTOVER ¾"CDX plywood. To get the same curve as the roof, hold a 12"x48" piece of plywood against the front edge of the roof and trace the curve with a pencil onto the plywood. Draw freehand a sawtooth, jagged edge (see plan, facing page) that measures 6" to 8" wide and cut along your pencil marks with a jigsaw.

Ask an assistant to hold the vergeboard in place while you screw it to the roof from above with 1½" deck screws. Attach the vergeboard to the front and back eaves.

STEP FIVE
GABLE DORMER

MAKE THE GABLE DORMER ACCORDING TO THE instructions on page 36. Paint a fake window and bars onto the front of the dormer, using your own spooky window design or copying the one in the illustration.

U.F.O. Playhouse

DEPENDING UPON YOUR IMAGINATION AND carpentry skills, this U.F.O. (Unidentified Fun Object) may resemble a rocket ship, a space capsule, an observatory or even a celestial spacecraft. Made of 2x4s and plywood covered with reflective mylar, it should take only two weekends to complete. It is sure to cause a sensation in your neighborhood, so if your neighbors can see into your backyard, it's a good idea to get their okay before you begin building. This is a great group project for a neighborhood playground.

MATERIALS

Quantity	Description	Size	Location
2	2x4 P.T. lumber	12'	base support
1 roll	perforated metal strapping	48"	base
4	4x4 P.T. lumber	8'	posts
1	1x2 #2 pine	8'	temporary brace, window props
2	2x8 #2 fir	10'	cross beams
1	2x4 #2 fir	14'	perimeter floor frame, hatch frame
1	2x4 #2 fir	16'	perimeter floor frame, hatch frame
2	¾" A/D ext. ply.	4'x8'	floor, ladder
2	2x4 #2 fir	10'	rafters
1	2x2 scrap ply.	9"	roof center post
4	½" CDX ext. ply.	4'x8'	roof
2	1x2 #2 pine	10'	window stops
2	½" A/D ext. ply.	4'x8'	tower sides
1 pint	flat black paint colored contact paper		
1 qt.	contact cement		
4 pairs	galv. hinges	1½"x3"	windows
4 pairs	galv. hinges	¾"x1½"	window props
60 lin. ft.	heavy-duty reflective mylar	27" high	

TOOLS

shovel
tape measure
level
framing square
speed square
chalk line
screwdriver
½" chisel
hand saw
staple gun
paint brush
portable electric circular saw
portable electric jigsaw
V.S.R. drill
Phillips head screwdriver bit
extension cord

NAILS, ETC.

1 lb.	10d galv. common nails
2 lbs.	8d galv. common nails
1 box	1¼" galv. deck screws staples

STEP ONE

BASE

To anchor the u.f.o. safely to the base, it is necessary to construct a strong subbase. Dig two 12"-deep 6'-long parallel trenches and two perpendicular trenches of the same dimensions so that a slightly smaller than 24"x24" square is formed inside the points of intersection. Cut the two 12' 2x4s into four 6' pieces, and lay one pair on edge in the bottom of two parallel trenches. Lay the second pair of 2x4s across them, forming a square that measures 24"x24". Join the pieces together with 12"-long pieces of perforated metal strapping by looping the metal strapping around the lower 2x4 and nailing it with 8d nails to the upper 2x4.

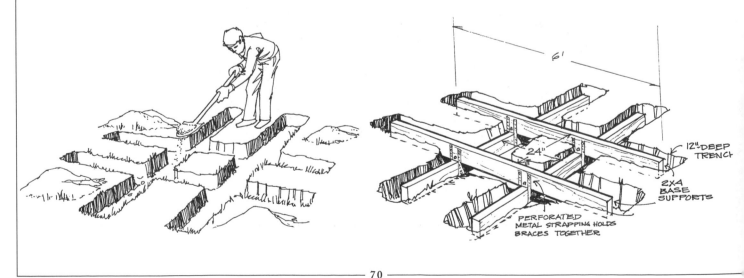

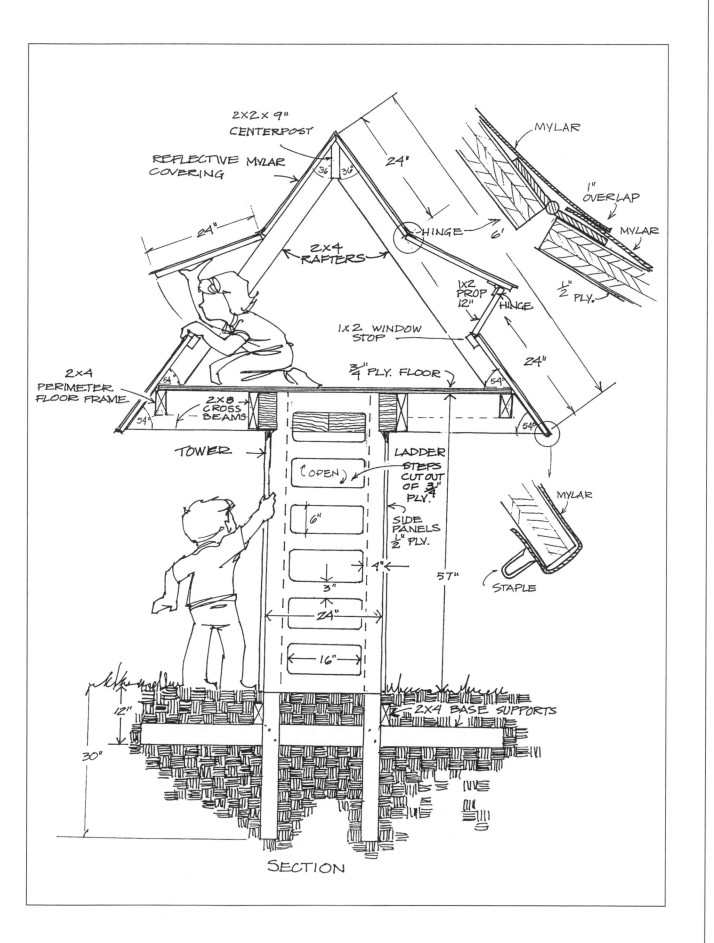

2x2x 9"
CENTERPOST

REFLECTIVE MYLAR
COVERING

36° 36°

24'

MYLAR

1"
OVERLAP

MYLAR

24'

2x4
RAFTERS

HINGE

6'

½ PLY.

1x2
PROP
12"

HINGE

1x2 WINDOW
STOP

2x4
PERIMETER
FLOOR FRAME

¾" PLY. FLOOR

54°

24'

54°

54°

2x8
CROSS
BEAMS

TOWER

(OPEN)

LADDER
STEPS
CUT OUT
OF ¾"
PLY.

6"

SIDE
PANELS
½" PLY.

4"

MYLAR

3"

57"

STAPLE

24"

16"

12"

2x4 BASE SUPPORTS

30"

SECTION

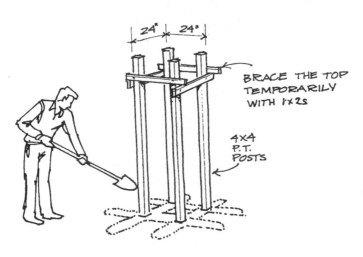

24" 24"

BRACE THE TOP
TEMPORARILY
WITH 1×2s

4×4
P.T.
POSTS

STEP TWO
POSTS

DIG FOUR HOLES, 6" IN DIAMETER AND 30" DEEP, inside the corners formed by the crossed 2x4s, and place the 4x4 posts in the holes. Nail the posts to the base support with 10d nails. To hold the posts in place, cut an 8' 1x2 into four 24" pieces and temporarily nail them around the perimeter of the posts with 8d common nails. Check for plumb and square and backfill the post holes and trenches, compacting the soil as you fill.

Mark and cut off the tops of the posts so they measure 57" from the ground. Using a hand saw and a chisel, cut a 1½"x7½" diagonal notch out of the top of each post.

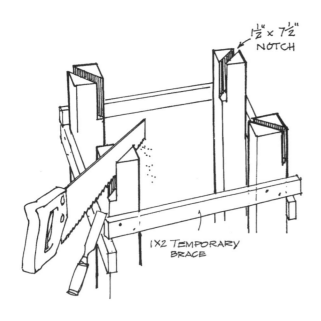

1½" × 7½"
NOTCH

1X2 TEMPORARY
BRACE

STEP THREE
FLOOR

TO MAKE THE CROSS BEAMS, CUT TWO 2X8S TO MEASURE 117" long, and cut out a 1½"x3¾" diagonal notch at their centers with a jigsaw. Fit the two 2x8s together and lay them into the notches made in the tops of the posts.

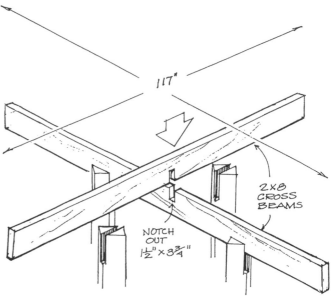

117"

2×8
CROSS
BEAMS

NOTCH
OUT
1½" × 3¾"

For the perimeter floor frame, cut the 2x4s into four pieces, and toenail them to the cross beams so they form a 6' square (see illustration, facing page). Remove the temporary braces and set them aside for later use as window props.

Cut the two ¾" plywood sheets in half lengthwise, giving you four 24"-wide, 8'-long panels. Cut off 24" from three of the panels, making them each 6' long.

Position the three 6'-long panels on the floor frame and nail the two outer panels to the frame using 8d nails, leaving the center floor panel loose. Save the leftover 2'x8' piece of plywood for the ladder.

Cut a 21"x 24" hatch cover out of the center panel as shown in the illustration and set it aside. Then, nail the center panel to the floor frame with 8d nails.

Frame the hatch opening on three sides with 2x4s, forming a ¾" lip to support the hatch door when it is closed. Cut a handhold in the hatch cover with a jigsaw.

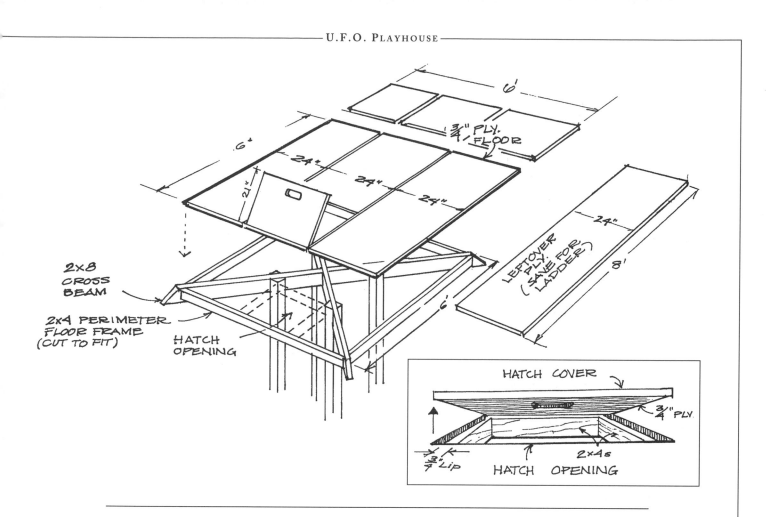

2x8 CROSS BEAM

2x4 PERIMETER FLOOR FRAME (CUT TO FIT)

HATCH OPENING

6'

6'

24"

24"

24"

21"

3/4" PLY. FLOOR

LEFTOVER PLY. (SAVE FOR LADDER)

24"

8'

6'

HATCH COVER

3/4" PLY.

3/4" LIP

2x4s

HATCH OPENING

STEP FOUR

RAFTERS

To form the rafters, cut two 10' 2x4s into four 5' lengths. Cut off the top ends at a 36-degree angle and the bottom ends at a 54-degree angle. Screw the top ends of the rafters to the 9"-long roof center post using 1¼" deck screws. Screw the bottom ends of the rafters to the floor also using 1¼" deck screws. Cut off the ends of the cross beams at a 54-degree angle, so they are flush with the top edge of the rafters.

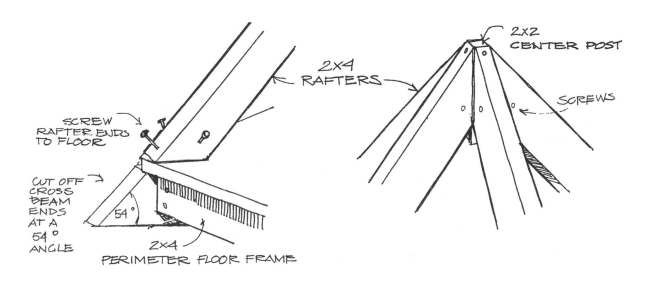

SCREW RAFTER ENDS TO FLOOR

CUT OFF CROSS BEAM ENDS AT A 54° ANGLE

54°

2x4 PERIMETER FLOOR FRAME

2x4 RAFTERS

2x2 CENTER POST

SCREWS

STEP FIVE
ROOF

UT THE SHEETS OF ½" EXTERIOR PLYWOOD TO THE following specifications:

Four pieces cut to 24"x 84" (first tier)
Four pieces cut to 24"x 60" (second tier)
Four pieces cut to 24"x 30" (third tier)

Starting flush with the bottom of the rafters, lay one of the 24"x 84" roof panels against the rafters, and mark and cut off the overlapping ends with a circular saw (as shown in the illustration).

Nail the panel to the rafters and the floor frame using 8d nails. Follow the same procedure for the other three sides of the roof. Repeat these steps for the second tier of roof panels, except do not nail this tier to the frame, for they will later be hinged and used as windows. Lay the third tier of panels above the second tier, then mark, cut and nail them to the rafters.

To make the window stops (see illustration, page 71), cut two 10' 1x2s into four 5' pieces and nail them to the bottom inside edges of the four window openings. Screw two 1½"x 3" hinges to the top outside of each window panel. For the props, cut eight 12" pieces of the 1x2 first used as temporary braces and hinge them to the bottom inside of the window panel using ¾"x 1½" hinges (see illustration, page 71).

STEP SIX
LADDER

SE THE LEFTOVER ¾" PLYWOOD TO MAKE THE LADDER. Cut it to measure 24"x57". Using a jigsaw, cut six 6"x16" footholds, leaving 3" between them. Round the edges of the footholds and sand them smooth.

Nail the ladder to the posts beneath the hatch opening. Then, enclose the "tower" by nailing three 24"x57" ½" plywood panels to the posts with 8d nails. Paint the tower flat black and decorate it with graphics cut from colored contact paper and applied to the sides.

STEP SEVEN
MYLAR

OVER THE TOP, MIDDLE AND BOTTOM ROOF PANELS and the three sides of the tower with heavy-duty mylar. Glue the mylar to the panels with contact cement. Fold it around the edges of the plywood and staple it to the inside of the playhouse. Overlap the top and bottom edges of the windows so rain will not leak in (see detail, page 71).

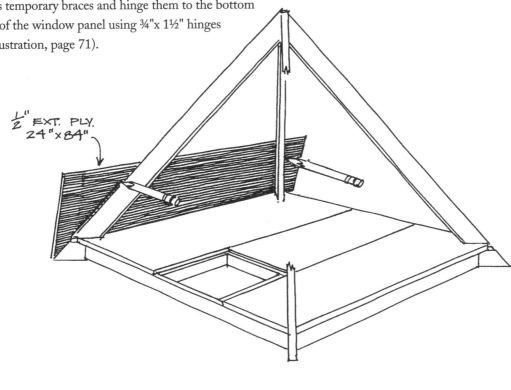

½" EXT. PLY.
24"x 84"

FUN HOUSE

HIS PLAYHOUSE IS DESIGNED FOR ACTIVE
kids and should keep them entertained outside for hours at a time. It can have as many play
activities as you care to include: a tire swing, a slide, the bouncing buoy, a cargo net and a sandbox
(see Section III for building instructions). The basic structure should take only a weekend to
make. Design it with your kids and add different activities as they grow.

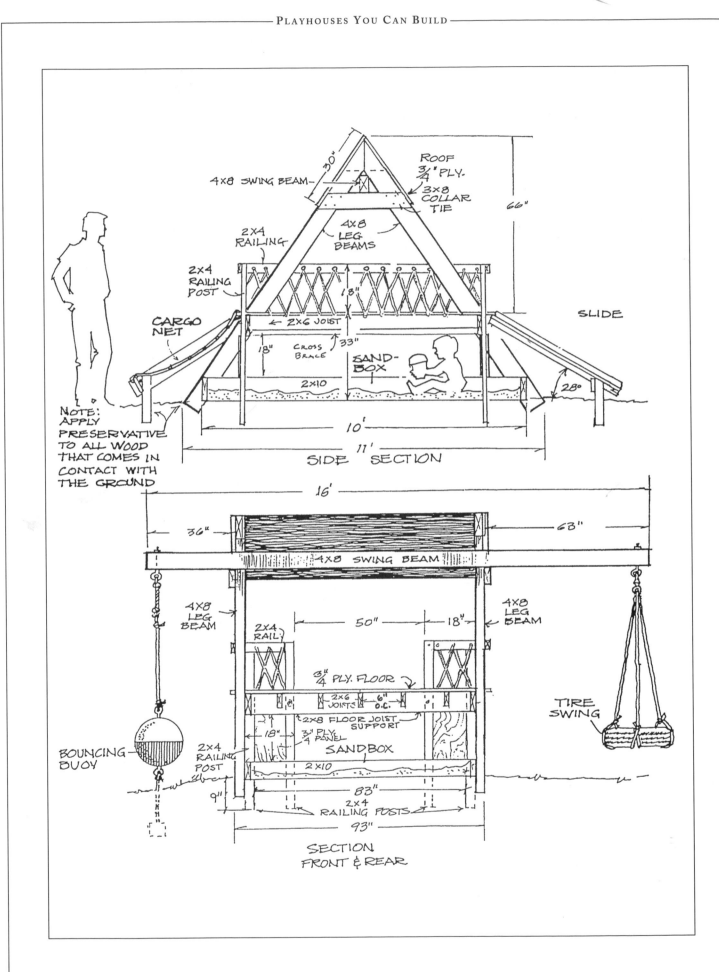

ROOF
¾" PLY.

4X8 SWING BEAM

30"

3X8 COLLAR TIE

66"

2X4 RAILING

4X8 LEG BEAMS

2X4 RAILING POST

18"

SLIDE

CARGO NET

2X6 JOIST

CROSS BRACE

33"

18"

SAND-BOX

2X10

28"

NOTE: APPLY PRESERVATIVE TO ALL WOOD THAT COMES IN CONTACT WITH THE GROUND

10'

11'

SIDE SECTION

16'

36"

63"

4X8 SWING BEAM

4X8 LEG BEAM

2X4 RAIL

50"

18"

4X8 LEG BEAM

TIRE SWING

¾" PLY. FLOOR

2X6 JOISTS

6" O.C.

2X8 FLOOR JOIST SUPPORT

BOUNCING BUOY

2X4 RAILING POST

18"

¾" PLY PANEL

SANDBOX

2X10

9"

2X4 RAILING POSTS

83"

93"

SECTION FRONT & REAR

M A T E R I A L S

Quantity	Description	Size	Location
4	4x8 #2 fir	10'	leg beams
1	2x8 #2 fir	14'	cross braces
1	3x8 #2 fir	8'	collar ties
1	4x8 #2 fir	16'	swing beam
4	¾" A/D ext. ply.	4'x8'	roof, floor, gusset plates
2	2x8 #2 fir	8'	joist supports
5	2x6 #2 fir	8'	joists
4	2x4 #2 fir	10'	railing posts
3	2x4 #2 fir	8'	railings
200'	rope	½"	guard rail
2	2x10 #2 fir	10'	sandbox (sides)
1	2x10 #2 fir	14'	sandbox (front & rear)
2 cu. yds.	sand		sandbox
16	galv. lag screws	⅜"x4"	
1 lb.	galv. common nails	6d	
20	galv. common nails	16d	
2 lbs.	galv. common nails	10d	

T O O L S

shovel
tape measure
level
framing square
speed square
hammer
vice grip pliers
½" chisel
ladder
chalk line
utility knife
portable electric circular saw
V.S.R. drill
Phillips head screwdriver bit
¾" & ⅜" spade drill bits
extension cord

STEP ONE

LEG BEAMS

FIND AN 8'X12' LEVEL AREA AND REMOVE ANY ROCKS, grass and tree roots. Lay two 10' 4x8s on the ground so the two top ends overlap and the two bottom ends are 11' apart. Mark and cut the top ends of the leg beams at an angle, then butt and nail them together with 16d nails.

Repeat these steps with the other two 10' long 4x8s. To reinforce the tops, cut four ¾" plywood gusset plates and nail them over the joints on each side where the leg beams meet with 6d nails. (To make the gusset plates, use the leftover plywood from the roof panels in Step Five.)

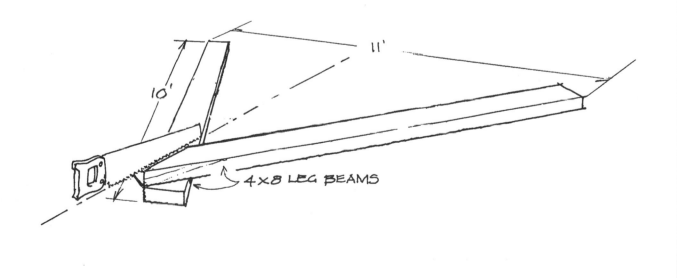

4x8 LEG BEAMS

CROSS BRACES

Cut the 14' 2x8 into two pieces, both measuring 7'. Without disturbing the position of the leg beams, nail this cross brace using 10d nails to the middle of each leg beam as illustrated. Repeat for the second cross brace.

COLLAR TIES

Cut the 6'-long 3x8 into two 36"-long pieces. Place one collar tie across the top of each pair of leg beams, allowing room above for the 4x8 swing beam to pass through. Nail the collar tie to the leg beams with 16d nails. Cut the collar tie ends off flush with the sides of the leg beams.

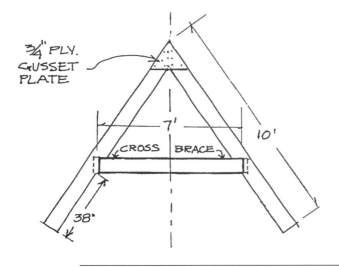

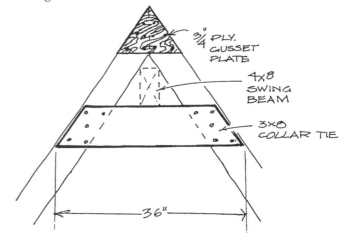

INSTALLING THE SWING BEAM

Slip one end of the swing beam through the space above the collar tie. Raise up and place one pair of the leg beams in position. With the help of an assistant, raise up the second leg beam assembly, again sliding the swing beam through the space above the collar tie. Adjust the swing beam so that it extends 36" from one set of leg beams and 63" from the other. Toenail the beam to the 3x8 collar ties and 4x8 leg beams with 10d nails.

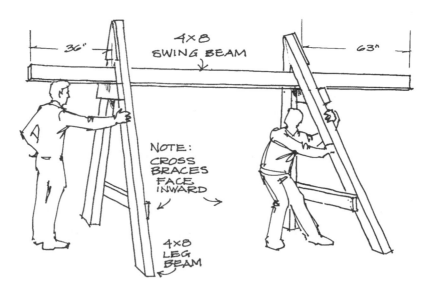

STEP FIVE

ROOF

To form the roof, cut two 30"x96" pieces out of the ¾" plywood. Position the plywood so that one piece overlaps the edge of the other (see illustration below). Nail both pieces to the top of the leg beams using 6d nails.

STEP SIX

JOIST SUPPORTS

To make the joist supports, cut two 86"-long pieces from the two 8' 2x8s. Nail them at the same height as the cross braces to form a rectangular floor frame.

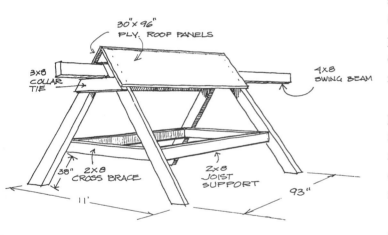

30"x 96"
PLY. ROOF PANELS

3x8 COLLAR TIE

4x8 SWING BEAM

38" 2x8 CROSS BRACE

2x8 JOIST SUPPORT

11'

93"

STEP SEVEN

FLOOR JOISTS & FLOOR

To construct the floor joists, measure the distance between the joist supports and cut five 2x6s to this dimension. Nail them to the joist supports at 16" centers.

Lay two sheets of ¾" plywood over the floor frame, notching out the corners with a circular saw to accept the 4x8 leg beams, and nail the plywood to the frame and the floor joists using 6d nails. Make sure the seam where the two sheets join lies over a floor joist. The plywood should extend past the frame on all four sides by several inches.

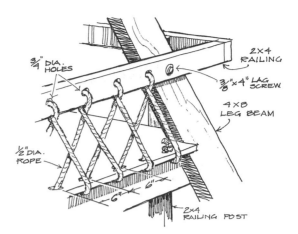

¾" DIA. HOLES

2X4 RAILING

⅜"x4" LAG SCREW

4X8 LEG BEAM

½" DIA. ROPE

6"x 6"

2x4 RAILING POST

STEP EIGHT

RAILINGS

To build the railing posts, cut the four 10' 2x4s into eight 5' lengths. Bury the bottom ends 9" into the ground. Attach a railing post to each end of the front and back joist supports, using one lag screw at each corner (see illustration, page 76). Chisel a notch out of the plywood floor for the railing posts. To frame the openings on the front and back, bolt each of the remaining four railing posts to the floor frame 18" in from the leg beam.

To construct the railings, cut the three 8' 2x4s into four pieces approximately 23" long for the front and back railings, and two pieces approximately 8' long for the side railings. Using lag screws, screw the side railings to the outside of the two leg beams and the front and back railings to the four railing posts.

Using a ¾" spade drill bit, bore holes approximately every 6" in the railing and the overhanging floor. Weave the rope through the holes to form a webbed safety guard.

STEP NINE

SANDBOX

To make the sides of the sandbox, nail the four 2x10s to the inside of the leg beams and fill the box with sand. To strengthen the base of the structure, cut four 18"x18" pieces from the remaining ¾" plywood, and nail them to the corner railing posts. There is just 18" between the sandbox sides and the floor frame above, but kids love to crawl in and play.

Tree House

THIS EASY-TO-BUILD TREE HOUSE WILL last for many years and can be enjoyed by children of almost any age. Escaping into a tree house can give a fresh perspective not only on the backyard but also on life. Our daughter used her lofty retreat from age three into her mid-teens. Even now (at 18), we'll occasionally catch her sneaking off there to read a book when she needs a break from the demands of school and home. There is something wonderful about being enveloped by tree boughs and maple leaves that lifts the spirit and centers the soul!

In addition to being relatively simple to construct, this tree house design will work in just about any tree. Choose a tree that is inconspicuous so as not to obstruct your neighbor's view. The tree should be about 12" in diameter with a fairly straight trunk. It should have no branches on it for the first 12'.

MATERIALS

Quantity	Description	Size	Location
7	2x6 #2 fir	12'	cross supports, perimeter floor frame, roof frame, ladder treads
2	¾" A/D ext. ply.	4'x8'	floor
2	2x4 #2 fir	10'	floor braces
2	4x4 #2 cedar	8'	corner posts
2	2x4 #2 fir	8'	knee braces
2	2x6 #2 pine	10'	corner rafters
2	2x6 #2 fir	8'	mid-roof rafters
2	1x8 #2 pine	14'	roof edge
8	1x4 #2 pine	12'	spaced sheathing
5 bundles	cedar shingles	18"	roof
1	2x6 #2 fir	14'	ladder legs
1	1x4 #2 pine	10'	ladder support cleats
1	2x4 #2 fir	12'	railings, railing supports
1	2x4 #2 fir	16'	railings
6	½"x½" molding	14'	railings
5	2x2 #2 cedar	10'	balusters

TOOLS

level
speed square
framing square
hammer
¾" chisel
hand saw
portable electric circular saw
V.S.R. drill
Phillips head screwdriver bit
⅛" spade drill bit

NAILS, ETC.

3 lbs.	6d galv. common nails	
2 lbs.	10d galv. common nails	
1 lb.	16d galv. common nails	
4	40d galv. common nails	
2 lbs.	3d galv. shingling nails	
1 lb.	8d galv. finishing nails	
1 lb.	4d galv. finishing nails	
1 box	1¼" galv. deck screws	

STEP ONE

CROSS SUPPORTS

CUT ONE 12' 2x6 INTO TWO 69" PIECES AND NAIL EACH one to the tree with four 16d nails. Nail each 2x6 5' up from the ground, so that the ends are equidistant from the center of the tree. Make sure they are level before nailing them to the tree.

Resting a framing square on the cross supports, draw lines at right angles on both sides of the tree trunk to mark where the notches will be located. Following these marks, cut two 1½"-wide notches halfway through the 2x6s.

Cut another 12' 2x6 into two 69" pieces and cut notches in them as you did in the first two beams. Fit these two notched beams into the other two notched beams to form a cross support. Before putting any weight on the cross support, take a couple of 1x4s from your lumber pile and nail these temporary braces to the two 2x6s that have their notches facing up (marked "A" in the illustrations).

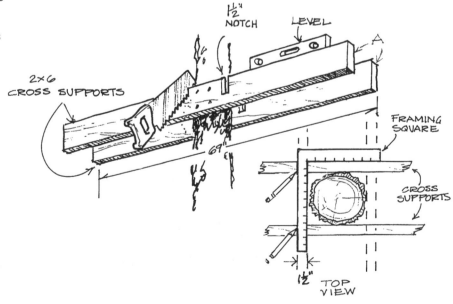

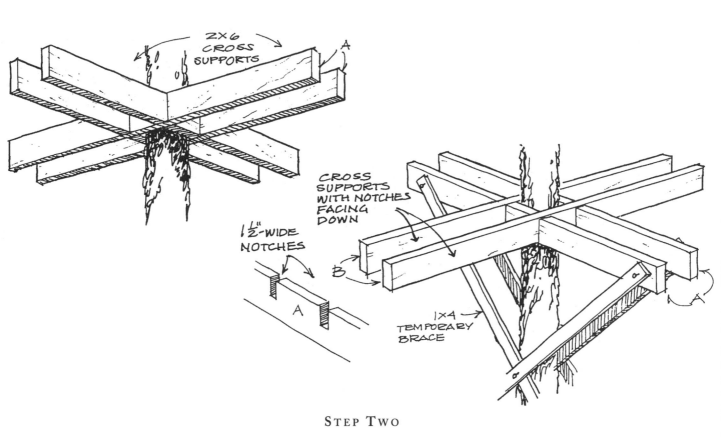

2X6 CROSS SUPPORTS

A

CROSS SUPPORTS WITH NOTCHES FACING DOWN

1½"-WIDE NOTCHES

A

B

1X4 TEMPORARY BRACE

STEP TWO

PLATFORM

To make the perimeter floor frame, cut a 12' 2x6 into two 69" pieces and nail them to opposite ends of the cross support with 10d nails. Cut another 12' 2x6 into two 72" pieces and nail them to the ends of the other cross supports and the ends of the 69" 2x6s with 10d nails.

For the floor, cut a 3'x6' piece from each sheet of ¾" plywood. For a strong floor, make sure the pieces of plywood run lengthwise in the same direction as the 2x6s marked "B." Using 6d nails, nail the plywood floor edges to the perimeter floor frame.

For the permanent floor braces, cut two 10' 2x4s into four approximately 55" braces to fit in the corners of the floor frame. Then, cut the ends off at approximately a 45-degree angle.

Chisel a small notch in the tree to support each floor brace (see illustration, next page). A notch this small will not hurt the tree; in fact, the tree will begin to grow around the joint in a few years.

Predrill a ⅛"-diameter hole in the permanent 2x4 floor brace and hammer a 40d nail through the brace and into the tree. Repeat for the other three braces. Then, remove the temporary braces.

6'

6'

B

A

2X6 PERIMETER FLOOR FRAME

1X4 TEMPORARY BRACES

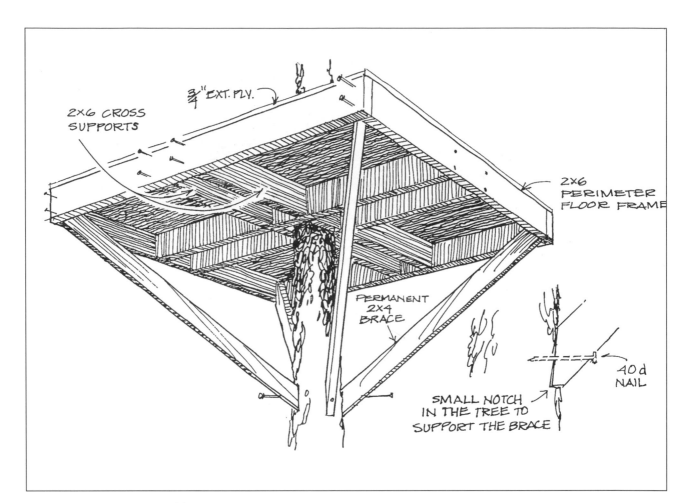

2x6 CROSS
SUPPORTS

¾" EXT. PLY.

2x6
PERIMETER
FLOOR FRAME

PERMANENT
2x4
BRACE

40d
NAIL

SMALL NOTCH
IN THE TREE TO
SUPPORT THE BRACE

STEP THREE
WALLS & ROOF

CUT THE TWO 4x4 POSTS INTO FOUR 42" LENGTHS AND toenail them ½" in from each corner of the platform. To build the roof frame, cut one 12' 2x6 into two 69" lengths and another into two 72" lengths. Nail them to the tops of the posts as illustrated using 10d nails. Then, construct the knee braces by cutting the two 8' 2x4s into eight 24" pieces. Cut the ends off at a 45-degree angle and nail them to the posts and the roof frame with 10d nails.

Cut four approximately 55" corner rafters out of the 10' 2x6s and trim the ends off at a 45-degree angle. Then, cut four approximately 42" rafters from the 8' 2x6s to fit midway between the corner rafters. Notch the ends of the mid-roof rafters that rest on the frame as shown in the illustration (facing page). Toenail the corner rafters and the mid-roof rafters to the roof frame and the tree with 10d nails. (Note: The dimensions given for the rafters are

estimates only. The dimensions will vary depending on the roof pitch and the diameter of your tree.)

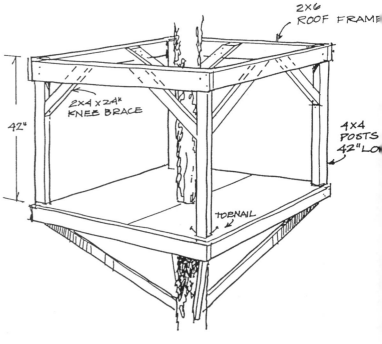

2x6
ROOF FRAME

2x4 x 24"
KNEE BRACE

42"

4x4
POSTS
42" LONG

TOENAIL

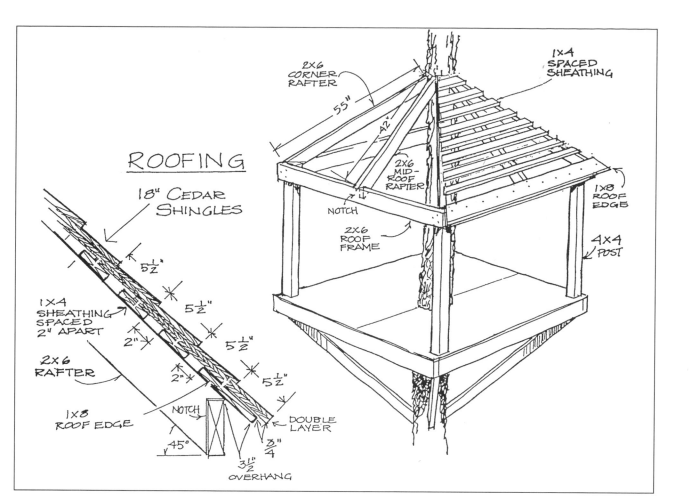

ROOFING

18" CEDAR SHINGLES

2x6 CORNER RAFTER

55"

42'

1x4 SPACED SHEATHING

2x6 MID-ROOF RAFTER

NOTCH

2x6 ROOF FRAME

1x8 ROOF EDGE

4x4 POST

1x4 SHEATHING SPACED 2" APART

2x6 RAFTER

1x8 ROOF EDGE

NOTCH

5½"

5½"

2"

5½"

2"

5½"

45°

¾"

3½" OVERHANG

DOUBLE LAYER

Around the perimeter of the tree house, nail a 1x8 roof edge board to the rafters and to the top of the roof frame using 6d nails, allowing it to overhang by 3½". Then nail the spaced sheathing to the rafters using 6d nails, allowing 2" between each 1x4.

Nail the shingles to the sheathing boards using 3d shingling nails, doubling the first course of shingles and allowing them to overhang the 1x8 roof edge board by ¾". Use only two nails per shingle, ¾" in from the sides and 6½" up from the bottom of each shingle. Also, stagger the joints of the shingles so they don't line up.

STEP FOUR

LADDER

FIRST, DIG TWO SMALL HOLES IN WHICH THE LADDER legs can rest. Then cut the 14' 2x6 into two 7' pieces for the legs. Position the bottom of each leg in the holes and rest the top of each leg against the top edge of

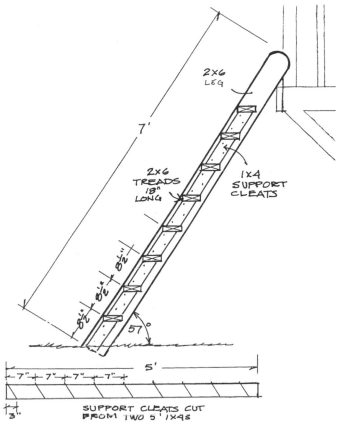

2x6 LEG

7'

2x6 TREADS 18" LONG

1x4 SUPPORT CLEATS

8½"

8½"

8½"

57°

7" · 7" · 7" · 7"

5'

3"

SUPPORT CLEATS CUT FROM TWO 5' 1x4s

the tree house floor. (Be sure to position the ladder so that it is in the center of the front of the tree house.)

Using a circular saw, cut eight 18"-long treads from the 12' 2x6. Then, cut 16 angled support cleats from the 10' 1x4 for each step as shown on the previous page.

Starting from the bottom up, screw two support cleats to the inside of the legs using 1¼" deck screws. (Use three deck screws per cleat.) Then, nail two 10d nails through the leg into the tread on each side. Continue this sequence until you reach the platform.

This ladder is heavy, but it can be removed by an adult if necessary.

STEP FIVE

RAILING

FOR THE RAILING AND THE RAILING SUPPORT TO THE left of the ladder, cut the 12' 2x4 into a 20¼" piece for the railing and a 19½" piece for the railing support. Then, nail the railing to the top end of this support. Use 8d finishing nails to nail the railing to the left corner post and the railing support to the floor. From the same piece of lumber, repeat the cuts for the railing and railing support to the right of the ladder.

Cut a ½"x½" molding strip to fit between the corner post and the railing support and nail it ½" in from the edge of the underside of the railing. Nail another ½"x½" molding strip directly below it on the floor.

Cut and nail 19½" 2x2 balusters to the railing using 4d nails and to the floor using 8d nails. Cut two more ½"x½" molding strips and nail them to the railing and the floor on the inside of the balusters.

For the railings along the other three sides of the tree house, cut the 16' 2x4 into three 62" lengths and continue installing the railing, balusters and molding around the tree house according to the plan.

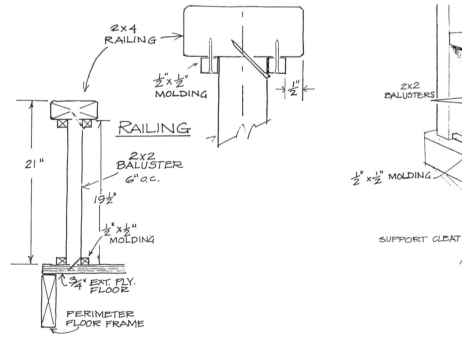

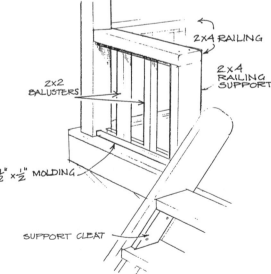

LOG PLAYHOUSE

THIS LOG PLAYHOUSE IS MADE FROM 8'-LONG landscaping logs that are sold at most lumberyards and nurseries in the United States. If you own land that is heavily forested with straight trees, you can cut your own logs using a chain saw. This is an ambitious project, however, and you may want to save time by giving the materials list to your local lumberyard and having them cut the logs to size. Since the logs you buy at the lumberyard are pressure-treated, there is little chance of the walls rotting. It is advisable, nonetheless, to keep the logs off the ground by building a low foundation with loose rocks.

An architectural symbol of the "wild west," this handsome playhouse deserves a cedar shake roof. Note that the roof extends over the front of the playhouse, providing protection from the rain and shade from the sun. The dirt floor is intentionally left unfinished (for rough and tough riders), however, a wooden floor would be nice for more citified cowpokes.

After your kids outgrow the playhouse, it can easily be turned into a tool or bike shed.

MATERIALS

(Dimensions given in parentheses refer to the finished [or cut] length of the logs.
It would be helpful to have the lumberyard precut these pieces to size.)

Quantity	Description	Size	Location
8	P.T. landscaping logs	8' [96"]	rear wall
7	P.T. landscaping logs	8' [88"]	rear wall
5	P.T. landscaping logs	8' [32"]	front wall
7	P.T. landscaping logs	8' [36"]	front wall
10	P.T. landscaping logs	8' [68"]	side walls
8	P.T. landscaping logs	8' [72" & 22"]	side walls
4	P.T. landscaping logs	8' [26"]	side walls
2	2x6 #2 fir	16'	door frame, window frames
3	2x4 #2 fir	8'	header
1	½" ext. ply.	4'x8'	header, gusset plates
5	2x4 #2 fir	10'	rafters
16	1x4 pine	10'	ridgepole, spaced sheathing
1	2x4 #2 fir	12'	nailers
4	1x8 T&G #2 cedar	8'	gables
1	1x8 T&G #2 cedar	12'	door
5 bundles	hand-split cedar shakes	24"	roof
4	1x6 #2 cedar	10'	gable trim, fascia boards
2	1x4 #2 cedar	10'	roof ridge trim
1	1x6 #2 pine	8'	door battens
1	1x6 T&G #2 pine	10'	shutters
1	1x4 #2 pine	8'	shutter battens
1	1x2 #2 pine	8'	door stop
1	1⅜"-dia. wood dowel	36"	pegs
2 pairs	strap hinges	10"	door
4 pairs	strap hinges	5"	windows
4	metal handles	5"	door
2	metal handles	4"	windows
2	slide bolts	4"	windows
	waterproof glue		

TOOLS

shovel
tape measure
speed square
framing square
hammer
level
¾" chisel
V.S.R. drill
Phillips head screwdriver bit
1⅜" spade drill bit
portable electric circular saw
extension cord

NAILS, ETC.

1 lb.	6d galv. siding nails	
1 lb.	10d galv. common nails	
1 lb.	4d galv. shake nails	
200	6" galv. spikes	
1 lb.	6d galv. common nails	
1 box	1¼"galv. deck screws	

STEP ONE

BASE

PREPARE THE SITE SO THE GROUND UNDERNEATH the inside of the house is slightly higher than the surrounding earth.

Mark the 6'x8' rectangular area where you want to build the playhouse and place a large flat rock at each corner. Adjust the rocks so they are level. Lay down the first layer of logs, butting the ends together where they meet at the corners. Make sure the bottom layer of logs is level and that the corners are square. They should form a 6'x8' rectangle.

Measure the diagonals from corner to corner. They should both be 120". Fill the space underneath the logs with stones of various sizes.

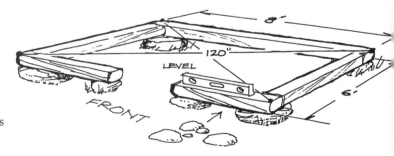

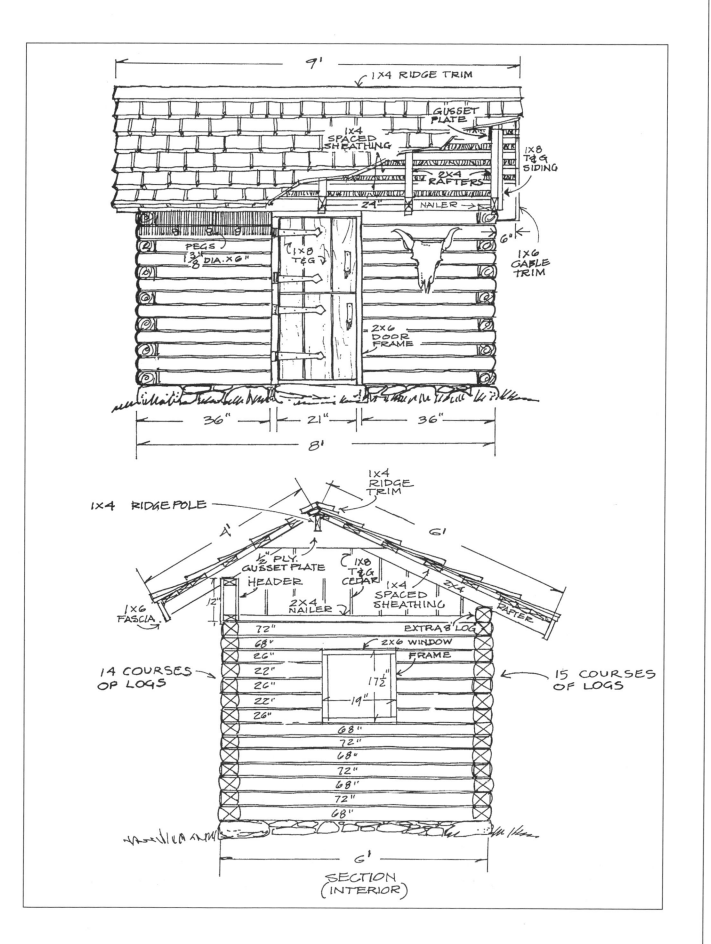

9'

1X4 RIDGE TRIM

GUSSET PLATE

1X4 SPACED SHEATHING

2X4 RAFTERS

24"

NAILER

1X8 T&G SIDING

6"

1X6 GABLE TRIM

PEGS 1⅜" DIA. X 6"

1X8 T&G

2X6 DOOR FRAME

36"   21"   36"

8'

1X4 RIDGE TRIM

1X4 RIDGEPOLE

4'   6'

½" PLY. GUSSET PLATE

HEADER

1X8 T&G CEDAR

1X4 SPACED SHEATHING

2X4

RAFTER

1X6 FASCIA

12"

2X4 NAILER

EXTRA 8' LOG

72"
68"
26"
22"
26"
22"
26"

14 COURSES OF LOGS

2X6 WINDOW FRAME

17½"

19"

15 COURSES OF LOGS

68"
72"
68"
72"
68"
72"
68"

6'

SECTION (INTERIOR)

STEP TWO

WALLS

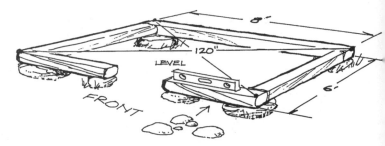

CONTINUE BUILDING THE WALLS, STAGGERING THE LOG ends as you build and nailing them together at each corner with two 6" spikes (see section drawing on page 89 for log lengths). Use one spike to nail the logs together where they meet the door and window openings.

After all the courses of logs are nailed in place, frame the door and windows with 2x6s cut to size.

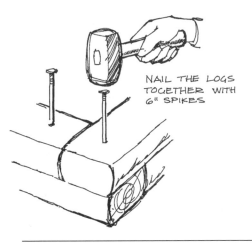

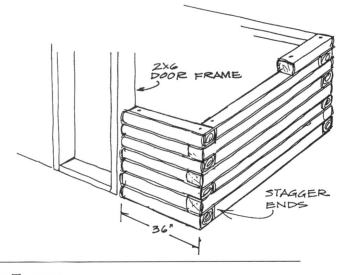

STEP THREE

HEADER

TO SUPPORT THE RAFTERS ABOVE THE FRONT DOOR, build an 8'x12" header out of 2x4s and ½" plywood as shown below.

Toenail the header to the top of the top front log. On the rear wall, add one extra 8' log.

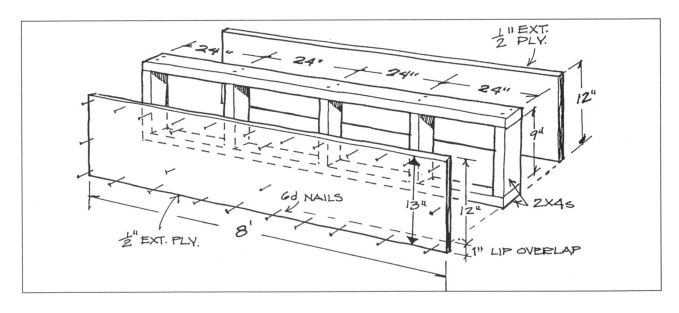

Step Four
Rafters & Gusset Plates

Cut the five 10' 2x4s into five 4' and five 6' pieces. Provide a notch for the rafters to sit on by cutting 1½"x2" notches 9" up from the end of the front rafter and 20" up from the end of the rear rafter.

Lay a pair of rafters on a flat surface so there is a ¾" space between the ends of the rafters at the top and 6' between the vertical faces of the notches at the bottom ends.

To make the gusset plates, cut a 6"-high x 18"-wide triangle out of the leftover ½" plywood to match the angle of the rafters at the peak and cut a ¾"x3½" notch in the top of the plywood as shown. Use this as a pattern to cut the remaining four gusset plates. Nail a gusset plate to each rafter pair with 4d shake nails. (Make sure the gusset plates face the inside of the log house.)

Construct the other three rafter pairs and nail on the gusset plates as described above. Then, lift both pairs of end rafters into position and temporarily hold them in place by nailing a 1x4 borrowed from the lumber pile into the rafter. Nail each rafter pair to the header and the top log on the rear wall with 6d common nails. Then remove the temporary brace.

Cut a 9' ridgepole out of the 10' 1x4. With a pencil, make a mark 6" from one end and then at 24" intervals until you reach 6" from the other end.

Make corresponding marks at 24" intervals on top of the header and the rear log. Mount the 1x4 ridgepole in the notches provided in the gusset plates, lining up the 6" marks with the outside edge of the two end rafters. Mount the remaining three pairs of rafters and center them on the 24" marks. Using 10d nails, toenail them to the top of the header and the top of the rear log. Finally, toenail the top of the rafters to the 1x4 ridgepole.

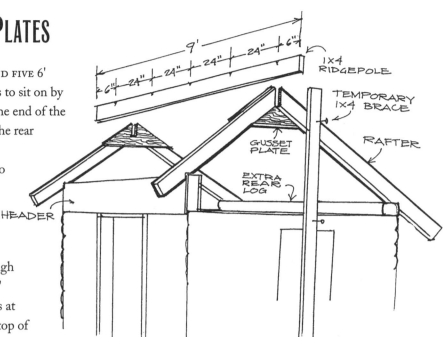

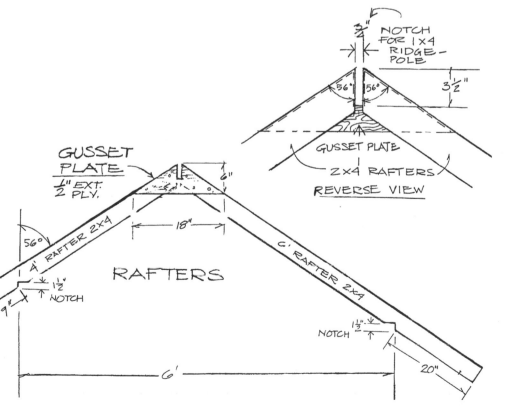

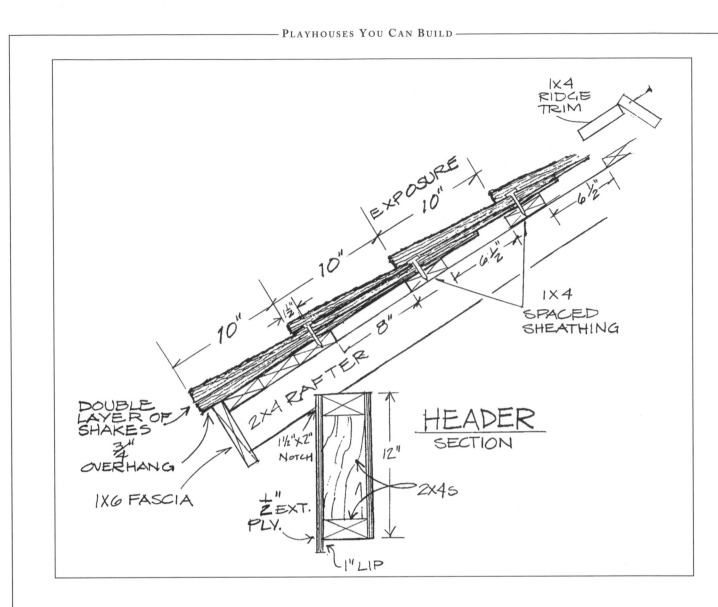

STEP FIVE

GABLES

INSTALL A 2X4 NAILER TO THE TOP OF THE LAST LOG ON each side wall. Cover each gable with vertical tongue & groove 1x8s, using 6d siding nails to nail the bottoms to the outside of the nailer and the tops to the rafter.

STEP SIX

ROOF

TO INSTALL THE SHAKES, FIRST COVER THE RAFTERS with 1x4 spaced sheathing cut to 9' lengths. Beginning at the bottom of the rafters, nail three adjoining 1x4s across the rafters. Leave an 8" space, then continue nailing

1x4s across the rafters every 6½" until you reach the peak of the roof. Make sure there is a 1x4 on both sides of the peak to support the ridge trim, even if there is less than a 6½" gap between the sheathing.

Next, install 1x6 gable trim to the exposed ends of the spaced sheathing and 1x6 fascia boards to the ends of the rafters. Nail both with 6d siding nails.

Make the first row of shakes a double layer. Nail two 4d shake nails 11½" up from the bottom of each shake, through the shake and into the 1x4 spaced sheathing. Cover the nail heads with the next row of shakes. (Hand-split shakes generally require 30# black felt paper between layers, but for a playhouse roof, this is unnecessary.)

After all the shakes have been installed, nail the ridge trim into the spaced sheathing with 6d common nails.

DOORS & WINDOWS

THE DUTCH DOOR IS MADE IN TWO SECTIONS OUT OF 1x8 tongue & groove cedar. The boards are glued and screwed together at the back using two 1x6 battens. Hang the doors with 10" strap hinges and provide 5" metal handles for both the top and bottom, inside and outside faces. For the door stop, cut the 1x2 to fit along the right side of the door opening and nail this piece to the frame with 4d shake nails.

Use the same construction techniques for the shutters, using the 4" metal handles and the materials shown in the plans, but window stops are not necessary. For hanging coats and other items, cut three 6" pegs from the dowel and install them by drilling holes with the 1⅜" spade bit.

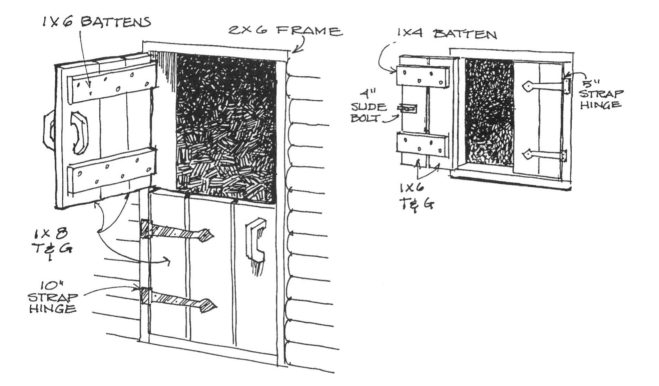

GARDEN TRELLIS PLAYHOUSE

AGE
RANGE
7 TO 12

CHOOSE A SUNNY SPOT IN YOUR GARDEN
for this playhouse, and build it at the end of a path, so it comes as a surprise when you encounter
it. This open-air playhouse, made of lattice and canvas, makes a wonderful garden retreat in which
your kids can practice being junior gardeners. They can get seeds started, put together bouquets
for tea parties or lemonade breaks, meet with their friends or just use it as a quiet place to read or
do their homework. Plant roses or clematis in front of the trellis walls and weave the stems
through the openings. After a year or two, this garden playhouse will look as if it is made of
blossoms.

The following instructions are for a brick and timber base; however, if you want to build a
temporary structure that can be easily moved, make the base out of pressure-treated lumber. (In
many locations, I have purposely used screws rather than nails, so the playhouse can be easily
taken apart and reassembled.)

MATERIALS

Quantity	Description	Size	Location
2	6x6 P.T. timbers	10'	base
½ cu.yd.	builder's sand		
100	used bricks	4"x8"	base
8	2x4 #2 fir	8'	posts
14	2x2 #2 cedar	8'	horizontal lattice frame, vertical lattice frame
4	2x4 #2 cedar	10'	top plates
2	¾" ext. ply.	4'x8'	roof
1	¾"x¾" quarter-round molding	8'	roof
1	12 oz. U.S. Army duck canvas, light (pearl) green with selvaged edge	6'x9'	roofing
2	1⅜"-dia. wooden pole	8'	roof
2	diagonal cedar lattice	4'x8'	walls
1	perpendicular cedar lattice	4'x8'	gables
12	1x4 #2 pine	8'	door trim, corner trim
1	1x4 #2 pine	10'	frieze board
1	⅞"x1⅛" nose & cove molding	10'	gables
2	11⁄16"x1⅜" solid crown molding	8'	gables
2	2x2 #2 cedar	12'	gable lattice frame brackets
½ sheet	¾" ext. ply. (marine-grade)	4'x8'	
1 gal.	contact cement construction adhesive		
1 gal.	semigloss enamel paint		

TOOLS

tape measure
framing square
speed square
wooden mallet
1" chisel
hammer
adjustable wrench
paint brush
level
caulking gun
staple gun
brick chisel
portable electric circular saw
portable electric jigsaw
V.S.R. drill
Phillips head screwdriver bit
straightedge
extension cord

NAILS, ETC.

1 lb.	3d galv. common nails
1 lb.	6d galv. common nails
1 lb.	8d galv. finishing nails
1 lb.	4d galv. finishing nails
1 lb.	2½" galv. deck screws
1 box	½" staples
8	40d galv. common nails
8	¼"x4" galv. lag screws

STEP ONE

BASE

BEGIN BY LEVELING A 5'x5' AREA AND REMOVING any large roots and rocks. Cut the 6x6 pressure-treated timbers into four 5' lengths. To join the four beams at the corners, cut lap joints as follows:

Adjust the saw blade so that it cuts halfway (2¼") through the beam. Starting at one end and continuing for 5½", make several cuts across the beam. Do the same for each beam end. Then, with a chisel and mallet, chop out the cut material to form an L-shaped notch.

Place the beams on the level site you have prepared, so that their ends overlap each other and form a 5' square. Check the diagonal distances between the corners, both of which should be 84¾". Drive a 40d nail into each corner and check the diagonals again for squareness. Then, drive four 10d nails into each corner joint to hold it in place.

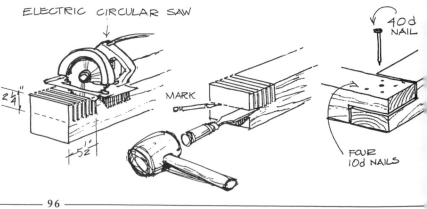

ELECTRIC CIRCULAR SAW

2¼"

5½"

MARK

40d NAIL

FOUR 10d NAILS

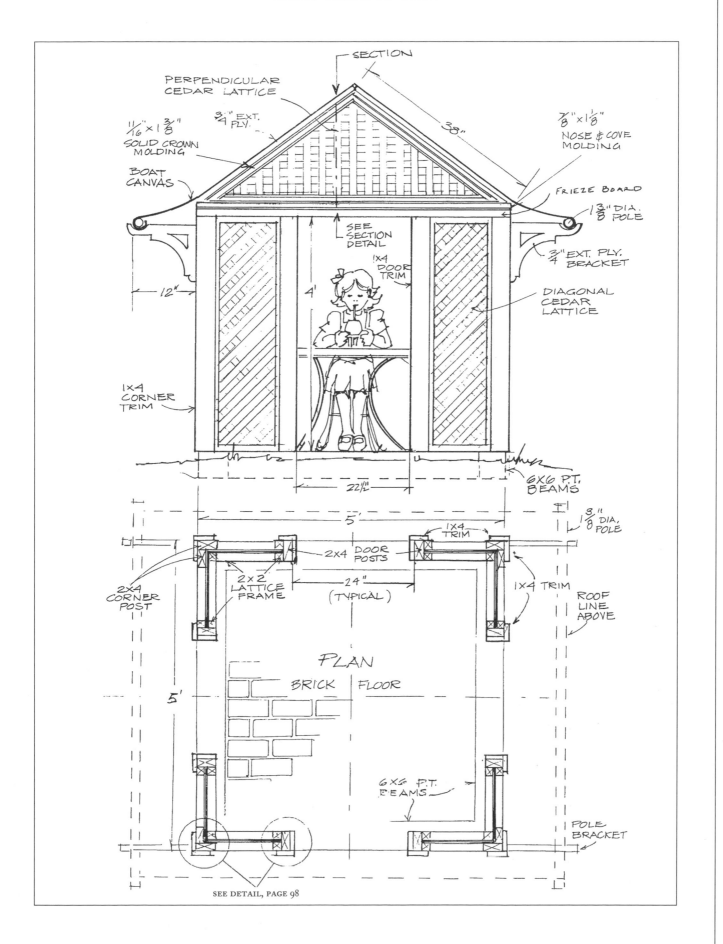

SECTION

PERPENDICULAR
CEDAR LATTICE

3/4" EXT.
PLY.

38"

7/8" x 1 1/8"
NOSE & COVE
MOLDING

11/16" x 1 3/8"
SOLID CROWN
MOLDING

BOAT
CANVAS

FRIEZE BOARD

1 3/8" DIA.
POLE

SEE
SECTION
DETAIL

1x4
DOOR
TRIM

3/4" EXT. PLY.
BRACKET

12"

4'

DIAGONAL
CEDAR
LATTICE

1x4
CORNER
TRIM

22 1/2"

6X6 P.T.
BEAMS

5'

1 3/8" DIA.
POLE

1x4
TRIM

2x4 DOOR
POSTS

2x4
CORNER
POST

2x2
LATTICE
FRAME

24"
(TYPICAL)

1x4 TRIM

ROOF
LINE
ABOVE

5'

PLAN

BRICK FLOOR

6X6 P.T.
BEAMS

POLE
BRACKET

SEE DETAIL, PAGE 98

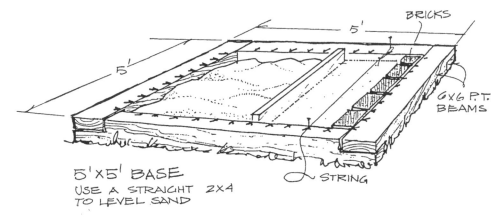

6×6 P.T. BEAMS

84 3/4"

5'

5'

STEP TWO

FLOOR

FILL THE SQUARED FRAME WITH SAND UP TO 2" FROM the top. Compress the sand as much as possible by packing it down with your feet. Use a straightedge to level off the top and sprinkle the sand with water before laying the bricks. To keep the rows of bricks straight, measure the width of one brick and mark two parallel beams with this measurement. Continue doing this for each row. Place a nail at each mark and connect the two nails with a string. Use this as your guide for laying the bricks. Stagger them as you go and, where necessary, use bricks that have been broken in half using a brick chisel and hammer.

BRICKS

5'

5'

6×6 P.T. BEAMS

STRING

5'×5' BASE
USE A STRAIGHT 2X4
TO LEVEL SAND

STEP THREE

WALLS

CUT EACH 8' FIR 2X4 INTO TWO 4' LENGTHS. USE TWO lengths for each corner and one length to frame each side of the entrance. To form the corner posts, screw two 2x4s together in an L shape (see corner detail). Stand one post up in the corner and screw it to the 6x6 P.T. base, using 2½" deck screws. Follow the same steps for the remaining three posts.

To stabilize the corner posts, construct a top plate by screwing two 2x4s to the top of the corner posts using 2½" deck screws. Overlap the 2x4s (see detail, facing page) and screw them together.

To install the lattice, cut and nail 2x2s to the outside edge of the framing using 8d nails.

(First nail in the vertical pieces.) Then, cut eight 14½"x48" pieces of diagonal cedar lattice and nail them with 3d nails to the 2x2s from inside the playhouse. Add a second frame of 2x2s on the inside to secure the lattice.

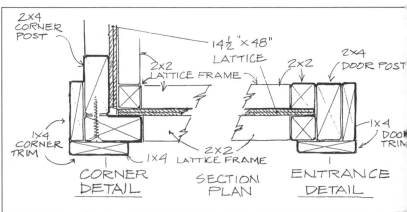

2x4 CORNER POST

14½"×48" LATTICE

2x2 LATTICE FRAME

2x2

2x4 DOOR POST

1X4 CORNER TRIM

1X4 LATTICE FRAME

2x2 LATTICE FRAME

1X4 DOOR TRIM

CORNER DETAIL

SECTION PLAN

ENTRANCE DETAIL

Step Three

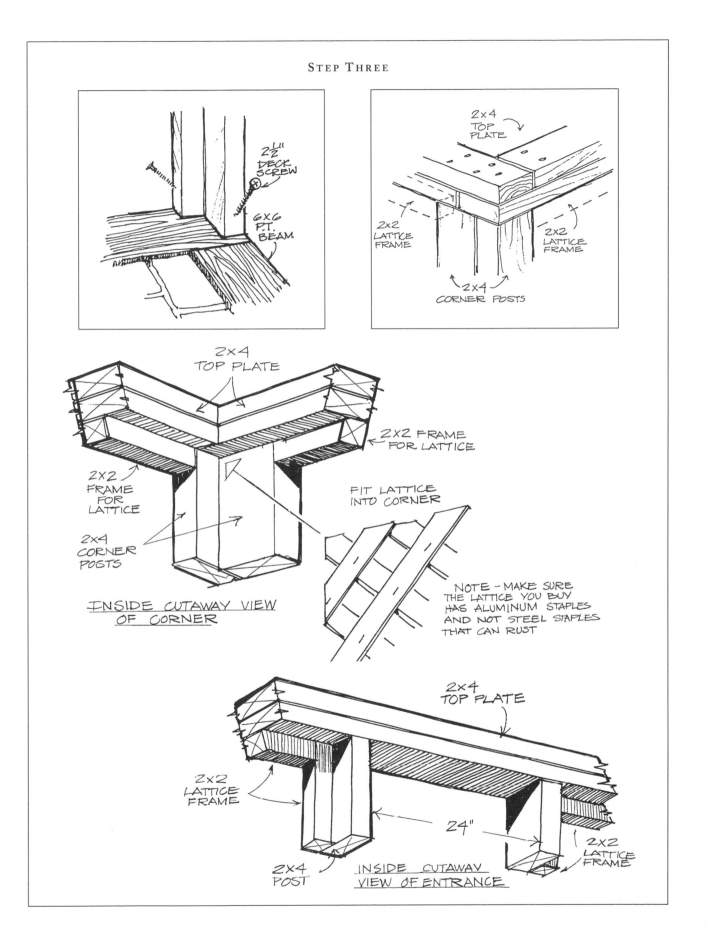

2½" DECK SCREW

6x6 P.T. BEAM

2x4 TOP PLATE

2x2 LATTICE FRAME

2x2 LATTICE FRAME

2x4 CORNER POSTS

2x4 TOP PLATE

2x2 FRAME FOR LATTICE

2x2 FRAME FOR LATTICE

2x4 CORNER POSTS

INSIDE CUTAWAY VIEW OF CORNER

FIT LATTICE INTO CORNER

NOTE - MAKE SURE THE LATTICE YOU BUY HAS ALUMINUM STAPLES AND NOT STEEL STAPLES THAT CAN RUST

2x4 TOP PLATE

2x2 LATTICE FRAME

24"

2x2 LATTICE FRAME

2x4 POST

INSIDE CUTAWAY VIEW OF ENTRANCE

STEP FOUR

ROOF

Cut two 38"x72" pieces of ¾" plywood. Lay one piece on top of the wall frame and, using 6d nails, temporarily nail the bottom edge of the roof panel to the top outside edge of the 2x4 wall framing. Make sure the short sides of the plywood overlap the frame by 6". Repeat this step with the second roof panel.

To make the roof assembly easier and to protect the canvas from chafing later on, use construction adhesive and 8d finishing nails to glue and nail a 6' strip of quarter-round molding to the top edge of one of the roof panels.

Standing inside the structure, and with the help of an assistant, push the panels up from the center until they meet at the top. (The temporary nails will bend and act as hinges.) Screw the bottom edges of the roof panels to the top plates with 2½" deck screws and remove the temporary nails.

Standing on a ladder outside the playhouse, screw the two top edges of the roof panels together with 2½" deck screws. Make sure the screw heads are embedded in the surface of the plywood.

Cover the roof with the piece of duck canvas that has had contact cement applied to one side, leaving an overhang of 1½" on each side. Next, apply contact cement to the circumference of the roof poles. Staple the overhanging canvas onto 75"-long poles and turn the poles, wrapping the canvas around them.

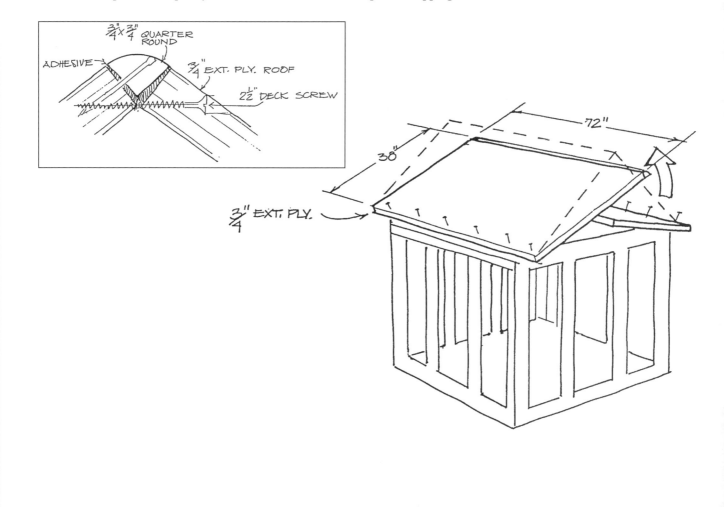

STEP FIVE

GABLE & DOOR TRIM

TRIM THE EDGES OF THE TRIANGULAR GABLE WITH solid crown molding. Nail two 1x4 frieze boards to the edge of the top plates using 8d finishing nails and nail nose & cove molding to the top of the board faces using 4d finishing nails. Cut one piece of perpendicular lattice to fit in each gable opening. Install the lattice from the inside and secure it with cedar 2x2s, toenailed on from the inside into the top plate with 8d finishing nails. Trim the other gable in the same way. Then, trim the corners and the four doorways with 4' 1x4 boards (see plan, page 97).

STEP SIX

BRACKETS

TO HOLD THE ROOF POLE, CUT FOUR BRACKETS OUT OF ¾" plywood as shown in the plans, using a jigsaw. Screw them onto the corner post trim, using ¼"x4" lag screws.

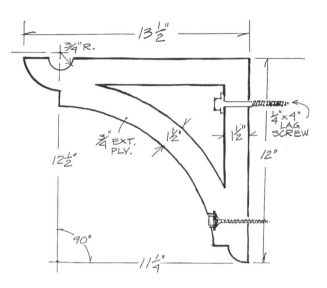

STEP SEVEN

PAINT

PAINT THE PLAYHOUSE WHITE THROUGHOUT. IT IS easiest to paint everything after the playhouse has been assembled.

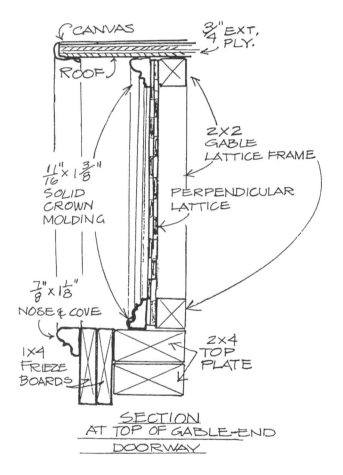

SECTION AT TOP OF GABLE-END DOORWAY

LEAN-TO PLAYHOUSE

THIS PLAYHOUSE REQUIRES PRACTICALLY
no man-made materials and can be constructed in just a few hours, using only a bow saw and
some rope. You do need access to a lush pine forest, however, preferably somewhere deep in the
woods, where there is a bubbling brook or a spectacular view. White pine is an excellent choice for
the roof and wall covering because it sheds water better than other species of pine. Balsam is best
for the ground cover because it forms a springy natural mattress and is aromatic.

An excellent camping lean-to, it is also a wonderful parent/child project. With a few minor
repairs each year, this playhouse will last a long time.

MATERIALS

50'-roll ¼"-diameter rope

TOOLS

bow saw

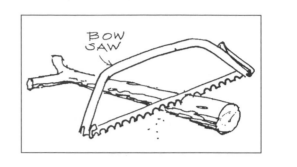

STEP ONE
SITING

LOCATE TWO TREES, APPROXIMATELY 8' APART. CLEAR the area between them of stones and roots, leaving a smooth, level space. If you are building your lean-to in a pine forest, spread a 4"-layer of pine needles over the earth for a soft floor. If possible, position the lean-to so the opening faces south to catch the sun's rays.

STEP TWO
FRONT FRAME

FIND TWO FALLEN TREES WITH A TRUNK DIAMETER OF 3" to 4" whose first branch fork is approximately 7' above the ground. Cut off the top of each tree right above the first branch fork. Find another fallen tree that is approximately 10' long with a 5" diameter. Rest it in the forks of the other two trees so it extends about 12" on either side of each fork.

STEP THREE
REAR FRAME

ADD FOUR 7' TREES TO THE REAR SIDE OF THE lean-to, lashing them to the top pole with rope. (Leave on any small branch stubs that point up, but cut off the ones that point down.)

REAR VIEW

STEP FOUR
REINFORCEMENT

ON THE FRONT OF THE LEAN-TO, LASH A 4"-DIAMETER cross beam to the two forked logs for reinforcement and to form an entranceway. Add three 3'-long "rafters," lashing them with rope to the cross beam and top pole.

To stabilize the lean-to, add two 30" posts to the main supports on each end as shown.

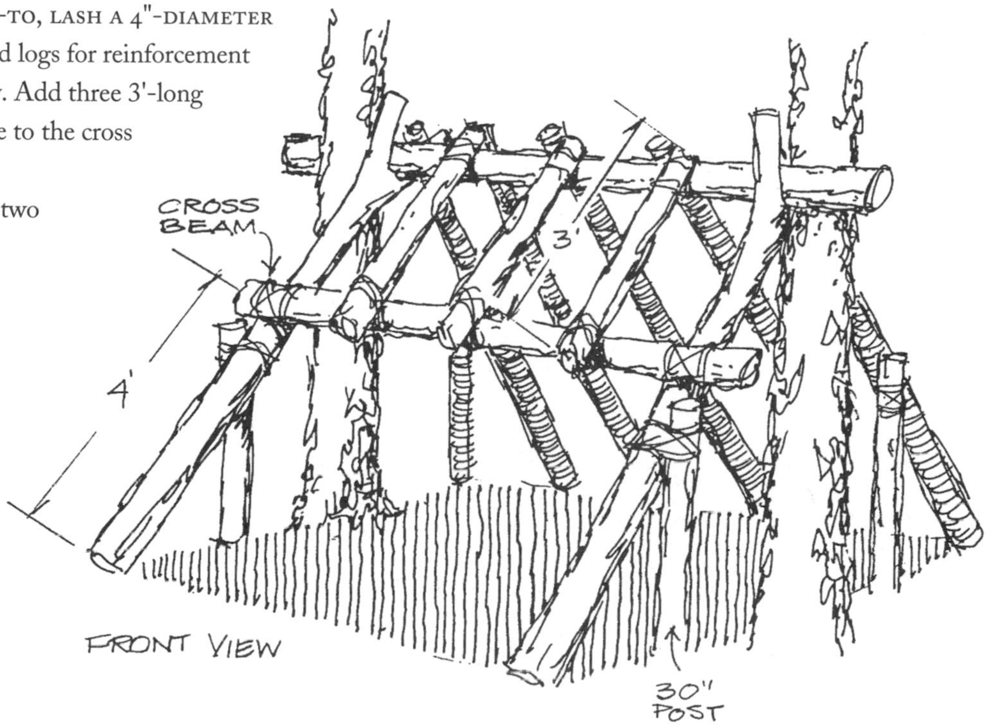

CROSS BEAM

3'

4'

FRONT VIEW

30" POST

STEP FIVE

CROSS PIECES

GATHER UP BUNCHES OF 1"-DIAMETER BRANCHES, approximately 3½' long, and weave them through the poles.

To finish off the lean-to, cut small pine boughs and hook them onto the cross pieces—camouflaging the hut so it blends with the forest, while still allowing a little sunlight to filter through in the morning.

PLAYHOUSE ACCESSORIES

BOUNCING BUOY

THIS SWING CAN BE AN ACCESSORY TO THE FUN HOUSE and attached to the swing beam (see p. 76) or it can be suspended from the branch of a tree and positioned at least 6' to 7' away from the trunk. To prevent it from swinging too far and bumping into its supporting structure, anchor the bottom to the ground by tying the buoy to a concrete block buried in the ground.

If you have a hard time finding an old buoy, you can buy one from a boatyard or order one from a nautical supply catalog.

MATERIALS

16"-dia. mooring buoy
3 galv. thimbles for ¾" rope
¾" nylon rope
(length depends on individual situation)
3 10"-long bungee cords
concrete block

TOOLS

utility knife

As shown in the detail, the buoy is suspended by a rope that is connected to a spring made out of bungee cords. The thimbles are spliced into the ropes to keep the ropes from chafing. To make the eye splice, consult a book on knots or seamanship.

ANCHOR ROPE TIED TO A CONCRETE BLOCK IN THE GROUND

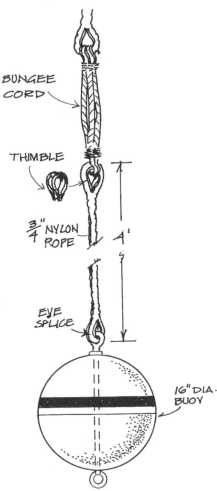

BUNGEE CORD

THIMBLE

¾" NYLON ROPE

1'

EYE SPLICE

16" DIA. BUOY

CARGO NET

You don't have to be a professional fisherman or a stevedore to make this net. It's simple to do and can be a fun Saturday project for you and your family. Playing on the cargo net is a good way for children to test their climbing skills. It can easily be attached to the Fun House (see page 76).

STEP ONE

To make the frame, cut the 10' 2x8 into two 56" pieces and the 8' 2x8 into two 48" pieces. Because of the amount of stress that jumping kids can put on the frame, make extra strong joints where the 2x8s join by chiseling out rabbet and dado joints. Screw the 2x8s together using three deck screws at each joint. Then, drill ¾" holes 8" to 9" apart for the ropes.

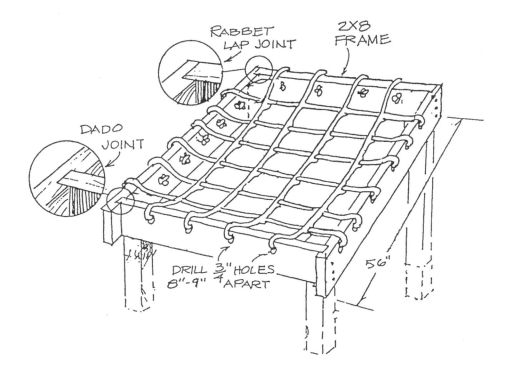

RABBET LAP JOINT

2X8 FRAME

DADO JOINT

DRILL ¾" HOLES 8"-9" APART

56"

MATERIALS				TOOLS
Quantity	Description	Size	Location	measuring tape
				¾" chisel
1	2x8 #2 fir	10'	frame	mallet
1	2x8 #2 fir	8'	frame	vise grip pliers
65'	dacron rope	⅝"		fid
1 spool	thin wire	24-gauge		propane torch
	4x4 P.T. lumber		support posts	magic markers
12	galv. deck screws	2½"		portable electric circular saw
4	carriage bolts	⅜"x4"		V.S.R. drill
8	carriage bolts	⅜"x5"		¾" spade drill bit

STEP TWO

Mark six 72" and four 80" lengths on the dacron rope. Tie the rope with light wire on either side of the intended cuts and cut the rope at the marks using a chisel and mallet. Seal the rope ends by melting them with a torch as shown in the illustration. Then, remove the wire.

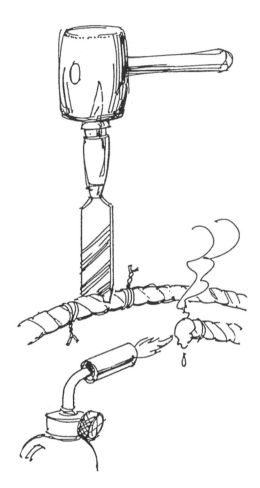

STEP THREE

Lay the ropes out in a grid and mark with a magic marker where they overlap. To keep the ropes in order, mark the ends of the horizontal ropes blue and the ends of the vertical ropes red.

Using a fid or a large nail, pry loose one strand of each vertical rope where it intersects a horizontal rope and feed the horizontal rope through this opening. Place the rope grid on top of the frame and wrap the ends of each rope over the sides of the frame and through the holes from the outside, knotting them on the inside. (There should be 12" extra on each end to allow for tying a knot.)

Once the cargo net is complete, lean it up against whatever play structure you have in the yard. Decide on an incline that your kids feel comfortable climbing on and bolt the leaning edge securely to the play structure using the four ⅜"x4" carriage bolts. Construct the support posts out of the 4x4 lumber as shown in the illustration. Be sure the posts are buried at least 10" in the ground. Bolt the frame to each post with ⅜"x5" carriage bolts.

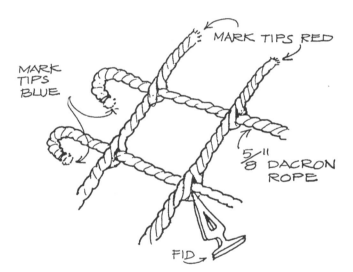

Swings

The "O" Swing

FOR OUR DAUGHTER, THE BEST SWING IN THE WORLD was her "O" swing. Made from an automobile tire, it was attached with rope to two trees near her tree house. She could swing to her heart's content, while still keeping an eye on her home away from home.

The tire is suspended by two ropes, enabling it to move in any direction, simultaneously spinning and swinging. This makes it much more maneuverable than the swings at playgrounds, which, because of their metal fasteners, are restricted to swinging only forward and backward.

For a really wild, dizzy ride, you can push the tire in such a way that it makes a figure-eight motion while spinning at the same time. Or, for those with strong stomachs, wind it up like a spring and let go—the tire will spin as it moves through its arcs. A favorite request of our daughter was to give her an "underdog," which required pulling the tire back slowly, as far as I could reach, and then, with a great push, running forward until the tire and rider were above my head and out of reach.

The "O" swing is also more sociable than the conventional single-seater, for three small kids can fit on it at once. And, while it can be made with very little money and effort, it provides children with hours of pleasure in their own backyards.

MATERIALS		TOOLS
1	discarded tire	utility knife
	¾" nylon or dacron rope*	hammer
	½" nylon or dacron rope*	
6	10d galv. common nails	

*Do not use polypropylene or hemp rope because both deteriorate when exposed to sun and rain.
Also, polypropylene is hard on bare hands.

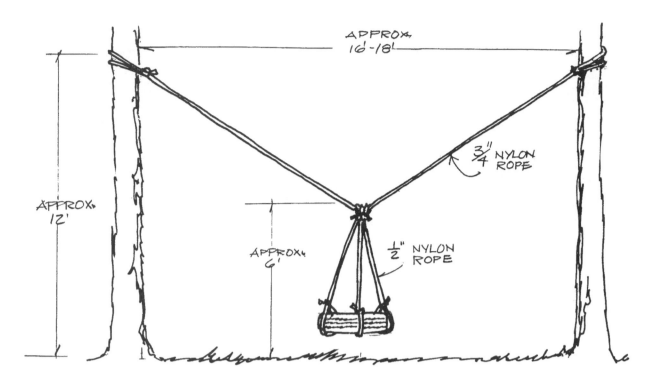

STEP ONE

Find two strong trees approximately 16' to 18' apart and at least 9" in diameter. Buy the ¾" rope in lengths sufficient to span the distance between the trees, plus 6' extra on each end, to allow for tying the knots. Using a ladder, attach the ¾" rope to the two trees, allowing it to sag 6' in the middle. Wrap the ends of the rope around each tree twice before tying it with a bowline knot (see below).

STEP TWO

Take three pieces of ½" rope of equal length and tie one end of each rope to the center of the ¾" rope and the other end around the tire at three equidistant points.

The top of the tire should be about 12" to 14" from the ground, depending on the age of the "swingers." Make it high enough so their feet don't drag on the ground, but low enough so they can stop the swing when they want to get off. Test the swing yourself, and when you are satisfied with the position of the ropes, hammer nails under the ¾" ropes to secure them to the trees. Hammer each nail half way in and bend it up to keep the ropes in place.

NOTE: Once the swing has been used for a while, the ropes will begin to stretch and will need to be adjusted periodically.

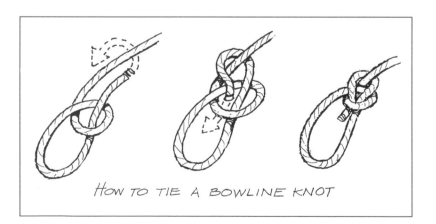

HOW TO TIE A BOWLINE KNOT

Traditional Swing

IT IS IMPORTANT THAT THE TREE YOU SELECT FOR this swing is alive and in good health. Find one with a straight branch that is at least 4" thick and approximately 9' to 12' off the ground.

STEP ONE

Cut the rope into two equal pieces and seal the ends with a propane torch (as described in the Cargo Net, page 110). Tie one end of each piece in a bowline knot (see page 112). Then, toss the knotted end over the tree branch. If this is difficult to do, tie a weight onto the loop, so it will drop down easier. Next, put the free end of the rope through the loop and pull, forcing the loop end up to the tree branch. (Make sure both ropes are in the correct position before tightening them, for they will be difficult to move once the loops are pulled up snug to the branch.)

STEP TWO

Make the seat out of a scrap piece of 2x8 cut to 14" in length. Take special care to sand the edges and sides until

MATERIALS
⅝" nylon or dacron rope*
(length depends on size and height of branch)
14" of 2x8 scrap lumber
medium-grade sandpaper

TOOLS

hand saw
V.S.R. drill
¾" spade drill bit
propane torch

Do not use polypropylene or hemp rope because both deteriorate when exposed to sun and rain. Also, polypropylene is hard on bare hands.

smooth. Drill a ¾"-diameter hole 1½" from each side of the seat. Pull the free end of each rope down through one of the holes and, after leveling the seat, tie the ropes off with a simple overhand stop knot. You can adjust the height of the seat by simply moving the stop knot up or down.

SLIDE

• •

Slides can be a lot of fun, but they can also be dangerous if they are not built with safety in mind. For instance, a slide should not be at a steeper angle than 28 degrees; otherwise, kids will shoot off the slide at uncontrollable speeds. It is also advisable to make a soft landing spot at the bottom of the slide, like a patch of sand. I also recommend not curving the bottom of the slide, since it does not really slow you down, and it can result in an unexpected lift at the end of the descent, often making it difficult for children to gauge where to plant their feet. Having a straight angle at the bottom also discourages kids from sitting on the end of the slide, where they can get hurt.

Make sure the rails are sanded smooth and are splinter-free. Use galvanized sheet metal for the sliding surface, and give it a coat of polyurethane every month or so. You can buy sheet metal from a shop that fabricates heating ducts. Ask them to cut the sheet metal to 48"x61" and bend 2" on each cut end to a 90-degree angle. Bolt the slide to a play structure (see Fun House, p. 75).

MATERIALS				TOOLS
Quantity	Description	Size	Location	hammer
1	1x6 #2 pine	10'	rails	tape measure
1	1x4 #2 pine	10'	rails	speed square
1	1x2 #2 pine	10'	rails	protractor
1	¾" ext. ply.	4'x8'	sliding surface	nail set
1	galv. sheet metal	4'x8'	sliding surface	vice grip pliers
1	1x4 #2 pine	8'	cross supports	V.S.R. drill
1	4x4 P.T. lumber	12'	support posts	¾" spade drill bit
1	2x6 #2 fir	8'	end supports	Phillips head screwdriver bit
1 box	galv. deck screws	1¼"		caulking gun
8	lag screws	⅜"x4"		2½" paint brush
4	carriage bolts	⅜"x4"		medium-grade sandpaper
	construction adhesive			portable electric circular saw
	polyurethane			

STEP ONE

Cut the 10' 1x6, the 10' 1x4 and the 10' 1x2 into two pieces, each measuring 54" long. Cut ½" from the width of the 1x4.

Glue and screw the pieces together with 1¼" deck screws as shown in the section drawing, leaving a 1" groove for the sheet metal and plywood panel, and cut off the top ends at a 28-degree angle.

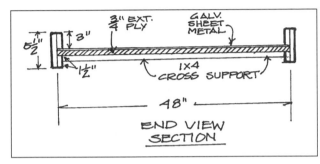

STEP TWO

Cut the ¾" plywood to measure 48"x57". For the cross supports, cut the 8' 1x4 into a 46½" piece for the bottom cross support and a 48" piece for the top cross support. Screw the cross supports underneath the top and bottom edges of the plywood with deck screws. (The bottom cross support is not as long as the panel is wide since it must fit between the rails.)

Place the sheet metal on top of the plywood so that the bent ends point downward and wrap the sheet metal around the top and bottom edges of the plywood.

Once the rails are assembled, stand up one side of the slide and fit the plywood and sheet metal panel into the groove. Then, fit the other

rail to the other side of the panel (using a helper). With a caulking gun, apply a bead of construction adhesive to the grooves where the panel and the rails meet. Then, screw deck screws through each rail into the panel every 6".

STEP THREE

For the support posts, cut the 4x4 P.T. lumber into two pieces measuring approximately 45" and two pieces measuring approximately 26". Cut off the tops of the 4x4s at a 28-degree angle.

Lay the two 45" 4x4s on the ground and space them 46½" apart, measuring from outside edge to outside edge. For the end supports, cut the 8' 2x6 into two 46½" pieces and screw one of them into the backs of the 45" support posts using lag screws. (Use a hammer and the vise grip pliers to start the lag screws into the wood, then continue turning the screws with the vise grips.) Stand up this assembly so that it is abutting the play structure and bury the posts 12" into the ground.

Fasten the other end support to the 26" set of posts. Then, position this assembly approximately 41" in front of the 45" support posts (measuring from outside edge to outside edge) and bury the posts 12" into the ground.

Screw through the side of the rails into the support posts, smooth the rail edges with sandpaper and coat the sheet metal with polyurethane. To fasten the slide to the Fun House, bolt carriage bolts through the end support on the slide into the 2x8 joist support on the Fun House.

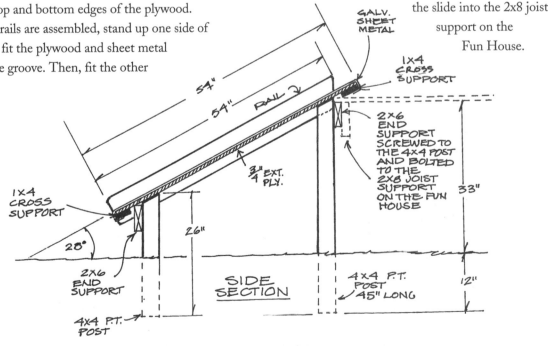

TROLLEY RIDE

● ●

FRIENDS OF OURS HAD THIS TROLLEY RIDE BUILT ON A wooded island in northern Minnesota, where they have a summer cottage. Traveling along a heavy cable about 50' long, it connected two treehouses and provided a sensational ride as well as a speedy way to travel from one to the other. The original was made from machined metal parts; I made my daughter's out of wood and designed a launching platform at one end, built from a piece of ¾" plywood.

To rig this trolley correctly takes experimentation and lots of rope! When buying your rope, measure the distance between the two trees, double it, and add an additional 10%. (If you use polypropylene rope, which is slippery and more economical than dacron rope, check it every year to see if it needs to be replaced. Exposure to sun and rain will cause it to deteriorate over time.)

Attach the trolley to the rope, and attach the rope to the two trees. Adjust the height and the length of the rope so there is a

MATERIALS					TOOLS
Quantity	**Description**	**Size**	**Location**		tape measure
2	marine-type single blocks (pulleys)				drawing compass
2	shackles	⅜"			hammer
	nylon rope	⅝"			adjustable wrench
	polypropylene or dacron rope	½"			portable electric jigsaw
1	¾" ext. ply.	4'x4'	trolley, steps		V.S.R. drill
1	#2 pine	4½"x11"	spacer		Phillips head screwdriver bit
2	Delrin sheaves*	2⅜" dia.with ⁷⁄₁₆" holes			⅜" & 1⅜" spade drill bits
1	¾" ext. ply.	4'x8'	platform, brace support		
1	2x4 #2 fir	8'	platform lip, back support		
1	1⅜"-dia. dowel	10"	handle		
10	#8 flathead screws	1½"			*Can be found at most boatyards
2	machine bolts with nuts & washers	⅜"x3½"			
24	galv. deck screws	2"			
12	galv. common nails	16d			
	wood glue				

safe descent. The speed and angle of descent is determined by the amount of slack in the rope. The more slack, the higher the rope must be on the tree, or the rider's feet will hit the ground. To prevent the rider from crashing into the tree at the end of the ride, attach the rope higher up on the tree to slow the trolley down to a stop.

STEP ONE

To make the trolley, cut two 8½"x13½" pieces of plywood from the 4'x4' sheet as shown in the plans.

STEP TWO

From the 4½"x11" piece of pine, cut out a triangular-shaped spacer according to the dimensions in the plan.

Glue and screw these three pieces together. (Sandwich the spacer between the two pieces of plywood.)

Then, drill two ⅜" holes, as shown, to provide axle holes for the sheaves and install the sheaves using the two ⅜"x3½" machine bolts and four ⅜" washers. Drill a hole for the dowel and glue it in place.

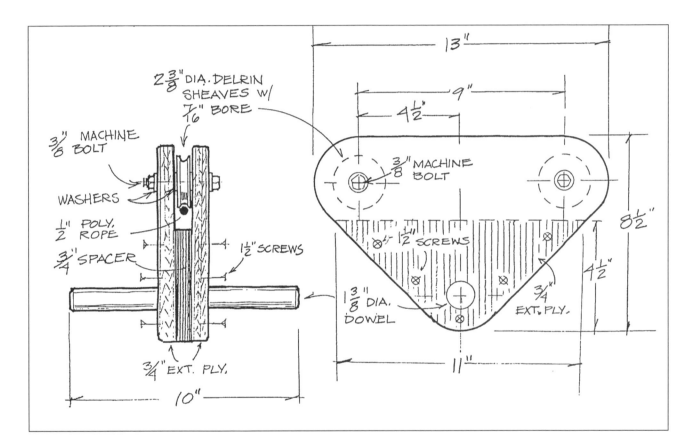

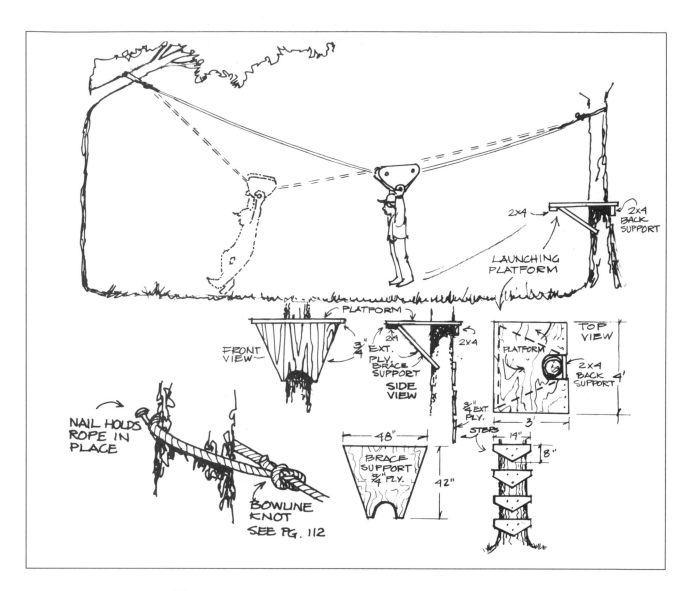

STEP THREE

To make the platform, cut a 3'x4' panel for the platform floor and an angled 42"x48" panel for the brace support (see plans) from the 4'x8' sheet of plywood. Then, cut a piece of 2x4 into two 4'-long pieces and screw one of them to the front bottom edge of the platform floor, while the plywood is still on the ground. The top of the brace support will rest against this 2x4 once the platform floor is in place.

Measure the diameter of the tree and cut a half circle of this diameter out of the center of the back of the platform.

Do the same for the bottom of the brace support.

Nail the other 4' 2x4 into the tree for the back support using 16d nails. With an assistant holding the platform against the tree, screw the back of the platform to the back support, then screw the bottom of the brace support into the tree while someone holds up the platform. Finally, screw the platform into the brace support with 2" deck screws. Use the leftover plywood from the 4'x4' sheet to make steps as shown in the plans and nail them to the tree using 16d nails.

SWAN ROCKING CHAIR

· ·

THE DESIGN FOR THIS ROCKING CHAIR WAS INSPIRED by the swan-shaped glass cups my mother served dessert in when I was a child. The dishes have long since disappeared but their graceful shape remains a vivid memory.

This project is fairly straightforward and should take only a weekend to complete.

If you decide to coat the swan with clear polyurethane, make sure you use an excellent grade of plywood, such as Baltic plywood. Some lumberyards do not stock high-quality grades, however, so you may have to special-order the wood.

MATERIALS			TOOLS
Quantity	**Description**	**Size**	tape measure
1	¾" A-A cabinet-grade ply.	4'x4'	portable electric jigsaw
1	1⅛" dia. dowel	10"	V.S.R. drill
	waterproof glue		Phillips head screwdriver bit
13	drywall screws	1½"	1⅛" spade drill bit
1 can	wood putty		5" sanding disk
	assorted sandpaper		rasp
	glossy enamel paint		chalk line
			C-clamps

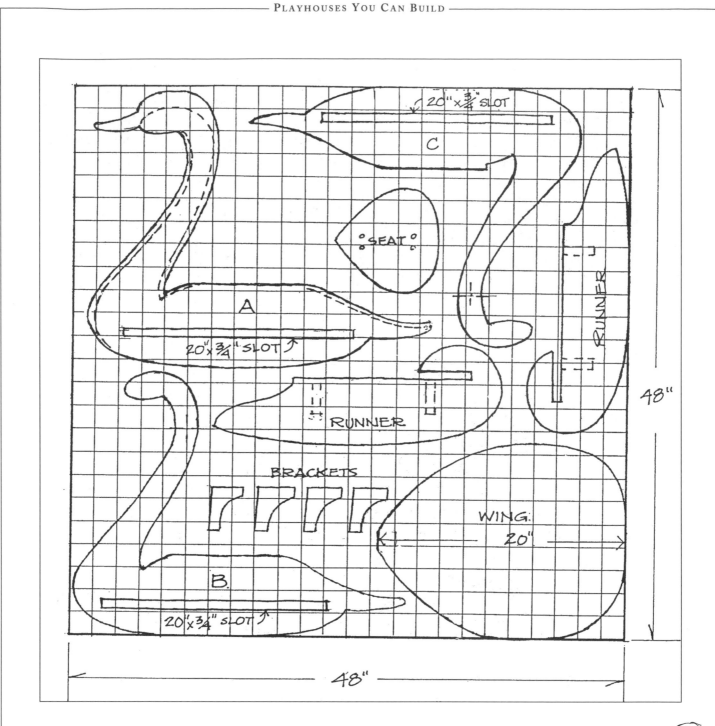

20" x ¾" SLOT

C

SEAT

A

20" x ¾" SLOT

RUNNER

RUNNER

BRACKETS

WING
20"

B.

20" x ¾" SLOT

48"

48"

STEP ONE

Lay out a 2" grid on the half sheet of plywood. Carefully draw the profiles of the swan as shown in the plan.

Use a jigsaw to cut out the pieces. Shape pieces B and C with a rasp. Then, using a drill with a coarse disk of sandpaper, smooth the edges. Fill any holes or gouges with wood putty.

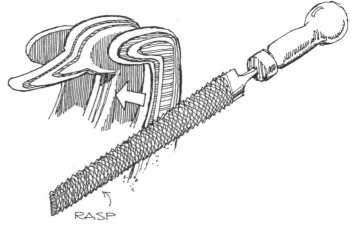

RASP

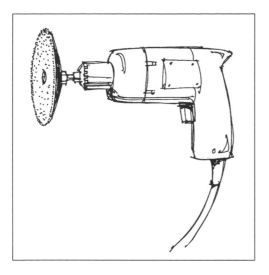

STEP THREE

Because the multiple layers (plys) of the wood make an interesting pattern, you may decide to simply coat the swan with clear polyurethane. On the other hand, painting it with several coats of glossy enamel gives you more options—white for the swan's body and black for its beak, or any color combination you and your child prefer.

STEP TWO

Glue and clamp pieces B and C to piece A and allow the assembly to dry overnight.

For the handle, drill a 1⅛" hole through the neck of the swan and insert the 10" dowel so that an equal amount protrudes on either side. Secure the handle with a drywall screw.

Slide the wings through the slot provided and glue in place. Slide the runners into place, then glue and screw the four L-shaped brackets to the underside of the swan's wings and the runners using eight drywall screws. See the cutting plan for the positioning of the brackets (shown as dashed lines on the runners). Glue and screw the seat to the back of the swan, using four drywall screws.

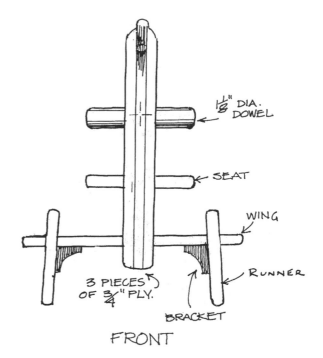

FRONT

PLAYHOUSE FURNITURE

N O PLAYHOUSE IS COMPLETE WITHOUT SOME FURNITURE for your children to use and rearrange. The pieces described here are sturdy, simple to build and require a minimal amount of materials. In fact, the table, which is a salvaged wire spool used by the telephone company, needs only some finishing work on your part to make it usable. Round off the edges and sand it down, then cover it with polyurethane or paint.

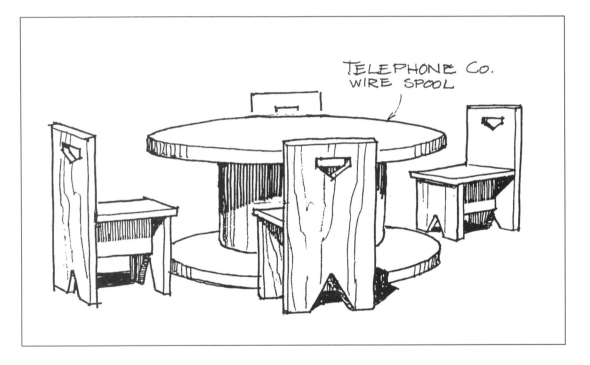

TELEPHONE CO. WIRE SPOOL

MATERIALS

Quantity	Description	Size	Location
2	1x12 #2 pine	8'	chairs
1	1x10 #2 pine	30"	bench
1	2x10 #2 fir	20"	bench
1	2x6 #2 fir	16"	bench
1 box	drywall screws	1½"	chairs
1 box	galv. deck screws	2¼"	bench
	carpenter's glue		
	medium-grade sandpaper		

TOOLS

measuring tape
speed square
portable electric jigsaw
V.S.R. drill
Phillips head screwdriver bit

CHAIRS

To make four chairs, cut the two 1x12s in half, creating four 4' pieces. Referring to the plans, cut these four pieces according to the dimensions shown. Join the pieces together, using glue and 1½" drywall screws.

Sand the surfaces until smooth and use as is, or coat the chairs with polyurethane or paint.

BENCH

Using the scrap 1x10 and 2x10, cut the pieces for the bench according to the dimensions shown in the plans. Join them together with glue and 2¼" deck screws.

Sand the surfaces until smooth and use as is, or coat the bench with polyurethane or paint.

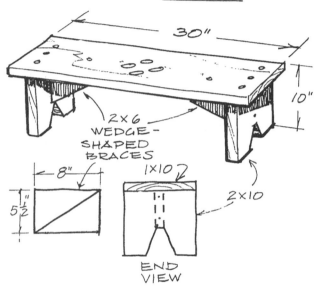

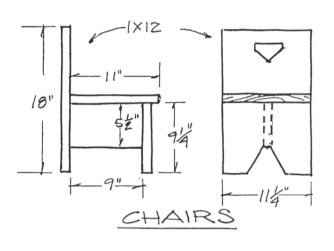

GLOSSARY

A/D plywood: Plywood that is clear or knot-free on one side only.

Baluster: A vertical support on which a railing rests.

Batten: A piece of lumber screwed across the back of doors or shutters to strengthen them.

Beveled cut: An angled cut.

Block plane: A small hand tool used to shave off or smooth lumber.

Butt hinges: Standard hinges.

CDX plywood: An inexpensive, exterior-grade plywood.

Chalk line: An instrument with colored chalk and string used to mark a straight line between two points.

Clapboards: Horizontal siding boards applied with an overlap.

Collar tie: A horizontal piece of lumber that connects rafters opposite each other and prevents them from spreading apart.

Contact cement: Rubber-based glue which adheres on contact.

Eaves: The overhanging edges of the roof.

Electric jigsaw: An electric table or portable saw used to make curved cuts.

Exterior plywood (ext. ply.): Plywood in which the plys are bonded together using exterior or waterproof glue.

Fascia board: A board nailed to the ends of the rafters, below the roof edge.

Fiberglass cloth: A cloth woven out of glass strands that is applied with polyester or epoxy resin.

Framing square: A large L-shaped metal measuring tool used when marking boards for framing.

Frieze board: The highest board directly above the siding and below the soffit.

Gable end: The triangular wall between the sloping ends of a roof.

Galvanized: A zinc coating used to prevent rusting.

Gambrel roof: A roof with two angled planes on each side of the ridgepole.

Gusset plate: A piece of plywood nailed over a joint to reinforce it.

Hardboard (trade name: Masonite): A brown sheet of building material made of compressed wood fibers.

Header: A horizontal support above window and door openings.

Joist support: A horizontal beam that supports the floor joists.

Lag screw: A screw with a hexagonal head that is used to join heavy pieces of lumber.

Lap joint: A joint made by lapping one piece of wood over another.

Light: An individual glass window pane.

Matte knife: A small, sharp-bladed, pointed knife often used to cut paper and cardboard.

Muntin bar: A strip that divides window panes.

Nail set: A small tool used to hammer nail heads beneath the surface of the wood.

On center: The distance from the center of one piece of lumber to the center of another.

Phillips head screwdriver bit: An attachment for an electric drill.

Pilot hole: A small hole drilled into a piece of wood to help prevent the wood from splitting when a screw or nail is driven into the wood.

Plate: Horizontal lumber on the top or bottom of a wall to which vertical studs are nailed.

Plumb: Absolutely vertical. Can be determined by using a level.

Pressure-treated lumber (P.T. or C.C.A. lumber): Lumber that has been chemically treated to resist rot and insects.

Rafters: Lumber that slopes from the roof ridge to the eaves and supports the sheathing and shingles.

Rail (window): The horizontal members of a window frame.

Rasp: A rough-edged file used to shape wood.

Ridgepole: A horizontal board at the peak of a roof, to which rafters are nailed.

Router: An electric tool used to cut grooves and shape lumber into various moldings.

Section: A drawing that shows the "cut-through" view of a building or object.

Selvaged edge: A fabric edge that is finished to prevent unraveling.

Shakes: Hand-split cedar shingles with a rough surface.

Sheathing: Boards nailed to the rafters before the shingles are applied.

Soffit: The underside of the roof overhang.

Speed square: A triangular-shaped metal tool used as a guide for cutting lumber at right angles with an electric saw.

Stile (window): The vertical members of a window frame.

Stringers: The main support for a staircase that holds the stair treads.

Structolite: The brand name of a lightweight plaster/cement.

Stud: 2x4 lumber used for vertical wall framing.

Toenail: To drive a nail through a surface at an angle.

Tongue & groove (T&G): Boards in which the tongue of one board fits into the groove of another.

Utility knife: A thin-bladed cutting tool used to cut shingles and other thin building materials.

Vergeboard: Decorative gable trim.

Vise-grip pliers: Adjustable locking pliers.

ABOUT THE AUTHORS

DAVID STILES is a designer/builder and the author of six
other how-to books, including *Sheds* and *The Treehouse Book*, which won
the ALA Notable Children's Book Award. A graduate of Pratt Institute and
The Academy of Fine Arts in Florence, Italy, he is the winner of two awards
from the New York Planning Commission for his designs for "The
Playground for All Children." His articles have appeared in
House Beautiful, *Popular Mechanics*, *American Home*
and *The New York Times*.

JEANIE TRUSTY STILES, a graduate of Wheaton College,
lives in New York City, where she is an actress/model and an instructor
of English as a Second Language at Baruch College. Jeanie and David have
a nineteen-year-old daughter, Lief Anne, who is a student at
Duke University. They divide their time between
New York City and East Hampton.